execute

execute

SELLING
IN A
DISTRACTED WORLD

JIM RYERSON

Cover Design by Chris McMorrow
chris@mcmorrowcreative.com

© 2019 by James Ryerson. All Rights reserved.
No portion of this book may be reproduced in any form, or by any means whatsoever, or stored in a retrieval system, or transmitted in any form or by any means (electronic, mechanical, photocopy, recording, scanning, or other, except for brief quotations in critical reviews or articles) without written permission of the author.

Ryerson, James, 1959 –

Other books by Jim Ryerson:

<u>Selling by THE BOOK Today</u>; Timeless Wisdom in a Referral-based World

<u>First 100 Days of Selling</u>, A Practical Day-by-day Guide to Excel in the sales profession

<u>First 100 Days of In-home Selling</u>, The Secret of the One-call Close

Dedication

Thanks to Jane, my wife and best friend of over 37 years. I can only imagine how challenging my lack of focus would be to live with on a daily basis, and she handles it all with grace, humor, and patience.

To my three daughters (and three sons-in-law) for providing me with so many projects to consume my boundless energy ("hyper-activity" is the clinical definition). It's so good to have all of you so near!

To the grandchildren, who cause me to smile with contentment and sheer joy every time I even so much as think of you. Having you nearby is the best distraction of all.

To God who gave me this brain with its unique set-up. Thank you for the vote of confidence to figure it out as I go through life, although it may have been easier had you provided me with an owner's manual (I guess you did…Philippians 4:8).

Table of Contents

Foreword i

Preface iii

Chapter 1: It's Not You 1

Chapter 2: It May Be You 11

Chapter 3: From Profession to Professional = SalesPRO 19

Chapter 4: PROfessor of Sales 25

Chapter 5: PROgram – The Power of 1 37

Chapter 6: A PRO is Found in PROcess 55

Chapter 7: PROmise = Let Your YES be YES 65

Chapter 8: The SalesPRO is PROactive 77

Chapter 9: The PRO is Found in PRiOrity 97

Chapter 10: PROductivity + Flow = SalesPRO 109

Chapter 11: PROspect & PROmote Go Together 133

Chapter 12: PROvide – Body, Brain & Energy 145

Chapter 13: PROgress vs Perfection 161

Chapter 14: PuRpOse – The Essence of "Good" 175

Chapter 15: The SalesPRO Will PROsper 187

Acknowledgements 195

Biography 197

Foreword

From 2017-2018 Jim Ryerson from Sales Octane, visited the Georgia, Carolina and North Texas BUILT chapters to discuss *Selling by the BOOK Today*. He shared the 8 waves of change hitting the world of sales and how to ride each wave by being "good" and connected.

The next challenge was how to implement the 14 characteristics of being "good" *and* grow your network at the same time. Getting things done is far more difficult now than in the past due to all the distractions we face. All indications are the distractions will increase so we need to learn some new habits so we can take control of our future.

EXECUTE: Selling In A Distracted World goes deeper into how to take control, learn new habits and master the skills necessary for each of us to build our referral stream while dealing with distraction. Everything shared in this approach aligns with the Core Values of BUILT: Leadership, Relationships, Trust, Knowledge, and Service.

Our sincere hope is that the content of the book and the message you hear during BUILT National will cause you to Think, Recharge your mind, increase your Connections with others all while you Plan for growth in 2019 and beyond.

It's time to EXECUTE!

Jeremy Greenwell
and
Matthew D. Marvel

BUILT NATIONAL

GROWING CONNECTIONS. BUILDING BUSINESS.

Preface

Salespeople are in the crosshairs. Increased customer expectations, escalating change in the marketplace, new technology to be learned and shiny objects pulling us in a multitude of directions all combine to create a cocktail of chaos. Chaos is a black web of distraction causing salespeople to move from one second to another as if being chased by a bear. Chaos is the enemy of Thought.

You used to call a customer and they would actually pick up the phone. If they did not answer the phone, a receptionist would take your message, wrote it on a pink "While You Were Out" slip and place it in front of your customer. You received mail once a day and you actually looked forward to receiving it.

Your customers stayed in their jobs for decades and were loyal by virtue of limited available alternatives. Your Rolodex was easy to maneuver and your day planner was loaded with check marks.

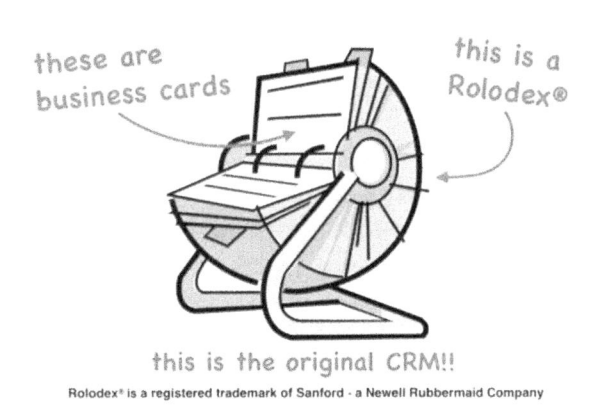

these are business cards

this is a Rolodex®

this is the original CRM!!

Rolodex® is a registered trademark of Sanford - a Newell Rubbermaid Company

You often had one person to talk to who could make the decision in your favor and you knew about their family and personal habits. Cross-state moves by your customers were the exception rather than the rule, so you often knew their favorite sports teams by virtue of their physical address.

In 2014, our book *Selling by the book Today* predicted the waves of change, shared the research driving those changes and challenged salespeople to be "good" and connected. The changes are happening just as predicted. Your customers change jobs more often, requiring you to constantly expand your connections within current customers. Technology has created barriers to initial engagement with prospective customers and gone is the helpful front desk replaced with a sterile phone in the lobby and a NO SOLICITING sign on the door. You have multiple emails, calendars, text, screen-sharing tools, conversation APPs, Facetime, mobile phone(s), a digital watch and everything works 24/7/365. You are always on! Artificial Intelligence tracks your every search, move and conversation, as iOT—the Internet of things—becomes more connected. Is this good news or bad news? It depends on your ability to embrace and master change—because change is guaranteed! For the Sales Professional, it is great news.

The Sales Professionals who embrace change and master a new approach to learning are adapting and accelerating their sales results while enjoying an improved quality of life. In <u>EXECUTE: Selling in a Distracted World,</u> we confront the chaos and provide the skills and techniques to break through and find the space necessary to EXECUTE.

We specifically address those changes impacting the selling profession. We start with WHY, and move to the WHAT, HOW and WHEN so you can break through the Chaos and create more space in your life.

And since this is a moving target, we'll continue to change as the days, weeks, months and years go by. You will have access to a site where you can continue to learn new approaches as we develop them in the years to come.

"Today you are either getting closer to or farther from the person you want to be"

~ Anon

    My guess is, you are reading or listening to this book because you want to improve. Regardless of where you are in your journey, this book will provide insight and specific techniques to help you accomplish that task. Then it's up to you to EXECUTE!

See you at the finish line!

Jim Ryerson
Chief Acceleration Officer
Sales Octane, Inc.

IT'S

NOT YOU

Chapter 1: It's Not You

Chapter 1

It's Not You

Like a batting cage with the automatic pitching machine turned up to full speed, the fastballs just keep coming. And then, when you figure out how to swing, it changes to a curve ball, and you start over. You don't even have time to think. It's the machine, not you. It seems impossible.

Prior to 1440 A.D., you learned either by someone physically talking to you, or you were one of the fortunate who had access to a handwritten document...AND you could also read (low probability).

Then the Gutenberg Press was invented and information sharing began its slow but gradual ascent. If you were one of the lucky ones who could read and had the means to own a book, you probably could only afford 3-4 books, which you read over and over and over again. There wasn't a lot of new information, other than what someone with a different book told you.

Then newspapers came on the scene, and by the mid 1800s, there were several hundred of them in circulation, thanks to improved printing presses. Then radio in 1920, which removed the requirement to read in order to learn. Television followed in 1930-1940 so you could hear, and more importantly, see new knowledge. Personal mobile phones arrived in the late 1970s, personal computers the early 1980s, smartphones early 90s, World Wide Web/internet 1990, first iPhone 2007, today it's Artificial Intelligence, Machine Learning, Simulation Gaming and the list goes on. This accelerates knowledge and is measured as "knowledge doubling." While this litany of interesting facts is fun to read it's a visual, which reinforces the point.

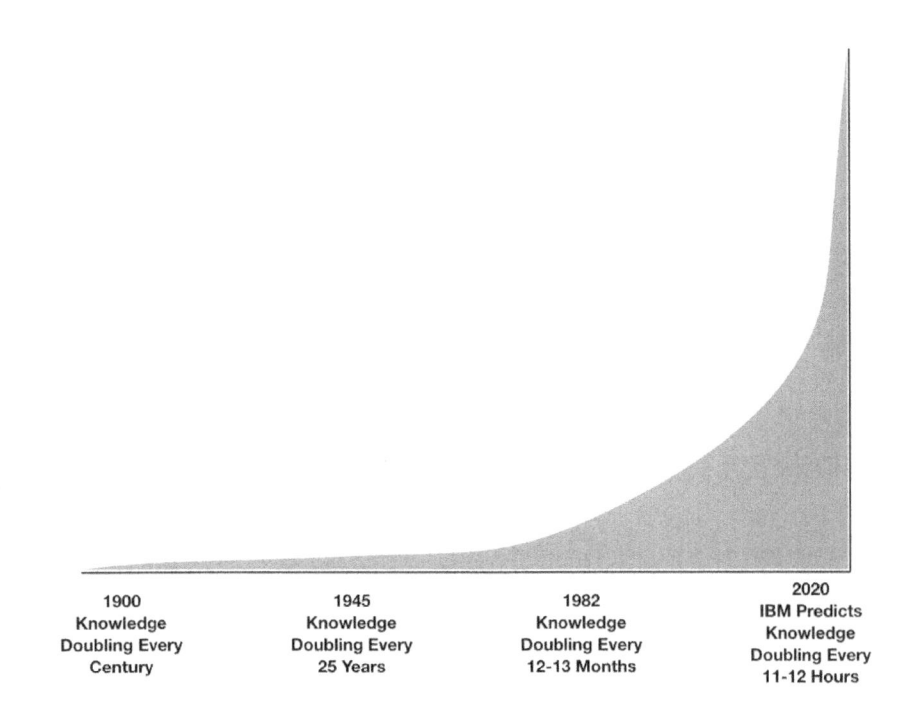

1900	1945	1982	2020
Knowledge Doubling Every Century	Knowledge Doubling Every 25 Years	Knowledge Doubling Every 12-13 Months	IBM Predicts Knowledge Doubling Every 11-12 Hours

The curve is alarming since more knowledge means more to learn. The more to learn, the more that is expected of us to know. Think of it this way. Customers have been to multiple sites to gather information before they reach out to engage with a salesperson. Once they choose to engage they expect the salesperson to add value. It's not you, customers require salespeople to have competence and competence comes from knowledge and the amount of knowledge is exploding.

When was the last time you picked up a new device or opened a new program or APP? It was likely faster and less expensive than a similar solution. This relationship between the advancement of speed of technology, lowering of cost and increased efficiency has been tracked over time using Moore's

execute

law. When you compare the speed, cost and efficiency of technology over time you will see the rate of improvement on a nearly vertical ascent. From the beginning of time until 1989 it was literally a horizontal line and then the technology explosion.

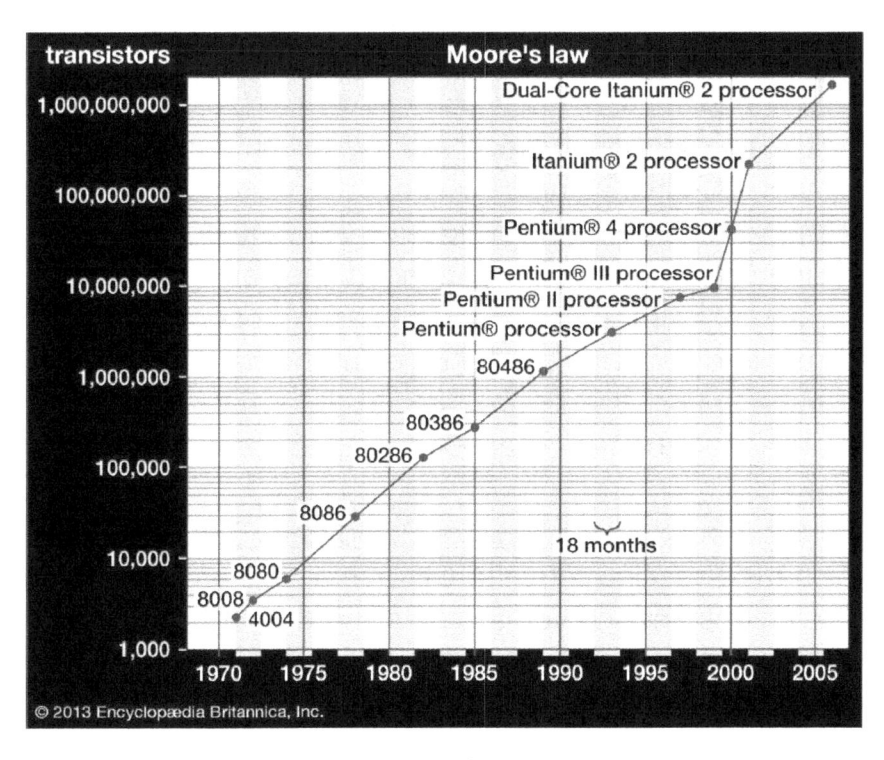

Moore's law

The good news is, you have technology with is faster. The bad news is it is most likely different from your current solution so you need to adapt to the changes. It's not you.

The next time you see the red notification on your digital device with an UPGRADE to an app, please take 30 seconds to glance at the fine print of what is included in the "UPGRADE." It begins with all the new features which are added in this free upgrade

Updates

and then near the bottom will be a litany of bugs, fixes, instability and crash-related issues which have now been addressed. In most cases you received a few "emoticons" in the UPGRADE as an enticement so the app will work better than before.

And once you upgrade something looks different. A button or feature that was not there before appears and the one you use is in a different place. You bemoan the fact you did the upgrade and begin to adapt to the new change. More change. It's not you.

Then distraction. Think about the last time you were sitting in a restaurant, catching up between appointments. Phones going off at the same time on both sides of you, and someone on the other side sharing a video of a concert they attended (at a very high volume) with their breakfast party. Look around the restaurant and see what percentages of the patrons, even those at a table with others, are staring into the glow of their smartphones. When does anyone get a quiet moment to think anymore?

In the book <u>Thank You for Being Late,</u> Thomas Friedman explains the shocking title: the ONLY time we are able to *really* think is when someone you are planning to meet is running late. Their late arrival gives you the only time where you have some margin in your hectic day when you can think. What do you do in those moments? Is your habit to grab your smartphone so you can see all the new things just added to your life?

I would argue that getting things done in the world of sales is more difficult than in any other profession because we have both external and internal customers. We are constantly interrupted with urgent requests and tasks from both sides, making it a challenge to focus on the important work we need to complete. External customers are more demanding than internal customers because they hold the purse strings. While a salesperson, similar to an employee, has a Manager and peers to

execute

deal with, the salesperson also has multiple clients and a sea of prospects and targets to wade through.

Change, increasing expectations, more change and no time to think. It's not you.

Jim Ryerson

Think It, Ink It!!

■ **WHAT**

■ **HOW**

■ **WHEN**

Submit your best practices at the link below for the chance to have it featured as a Shot of Octane Video.
https://salesoctane.com/resources/best-practices/

IT MAY

BE YOU

Chapter 2: It May Be You

Chapter 2

It May Be You

How often do you multi-task? How often do you check email, text, social media or your phone messages? As a percentage, how many tasks do you complete from start to finish without being diverted? (Other questions pertaining to the paragraphs below?) If you feel a bit guilty, be assured: you are in good company.

In the summer of 2017, I went to a neurologist/psychologist to get evaluated for what is often referred to as "shiny object" or "squirrel" syndrome. Everyone told me I had had "it" for decades. Thankfully, I had time in my schedule over the summer, so I could go to the professionals. After numerous evaluations, tests and assessments, the outcome was positive! I was clinically diagnosed with Attention Deficit / Hyperactivity Disorder. This is one of those times when positive is not so good.

I'm not alone. Since 2010, our company, Sales Octane, have been testing salespeople with a tool to determine how they behave in a selling situation. Over that span of time, we assessed over 6,700 (and counting!) salespeople.

From the start, we noticed a pattern emerging in the results. The largest percentage of salespeople—a disproportionate amount compared to the norm—had two common characteristics. And these two characteristics are prone to being drawn toward and distracted by shiny objects and passing squirrels. One of these two characteristics was an extroverted vs. introverted tendency. In some cases they were

Jim Ryerson

Ambiverts, a mix of the two, but a much lower percentage were introverts. Second, we found a higher than normal people orientation vs. a task/detail orientation.

This makes sense. Hire salespeople who get their energy from being around other people (hopefully customers and prospects), a classic definition of extroversion. Or hire people who are people-oriented to draw customers and prospects based on the salespersons people-oriented skills.

The flip side of the coin is oftentimes this behavior style carries with it the need for the individual to be liked, by customers and prospects. Not a bad characteristic if managed. If unmanaged, however, it can become non-stop overcommitting, driven by a need to be liked.

Eerily absent in a disproportionate number of the salespeople we assessed was a dominant Task/Detail orientation. Again, this makes sense— the Task/Detail frequently aligns with an Analytical bent. 5 out of 4 salespeople are terrible at math and statistics.

When you take a fear of being disliked, combine it with a lack of detail orientation and add in an attraction towards shiny objects, you have the perfect ingredients for a cocktail of chaos.

So, it may *also* be you. It makes sense that salespeople would feel more challenged in this new world. You may feel like you are busier than ever before. The word "busy-ness" sounds just like business and busy-ness often masquerades itself as business for too many salespeople. They hectically run from one issue to another, embracing the mantra of Nike, the Greek god of Victory: JUST DO IT! Maybe we need to THINK before we JUST DO IT.

Thinking demands replacing Chaos with White Space

execute

Whether it's the world around us or the world within us, we must be able to think in order to manage the Chaos around us. We often resort to our need for more time. If we had more time we could think and manage the chaos. One has only to look around to realize we all have the same amount of time and some salespeople accomplish much more than others and often in less time. They have cut through the Chaos and developed an approach that allows them to think and EXECUTE at a higher level. They have mastered the creation and use of what we will call "white space."

"White space" is a visual arts term meant to describe the unused space in any graphic representation. This could be a billboard, marketing piece, virtually anything created by someone in the graphics profession. It's white space—nothing is happening there. In advertising you want to use as much of this space as possible, because the only reason to have white space is to serve as a background to the graphic intended to be seen.

Unfortunately, salespeople have taken the same approach to "white space." We leave no time to think, filling every second of every minute and every space with activity. Our brain is racing nonstop with things we need to do, things we forgot, things we want to do yet have no time to do. We need time to think. Our brains need some white space.

On brain scans, the overactive areas are always filled with color. The peaceful area of the brain scan is white. We need more "white space" in our brains, calendars and life in order to think. Yes, it's counterintuitive, but it is the key to EXECUTE and moving from "good" to "great." To manage Chaos, you need to create "white space." Space to think, space to focus, space in time. Think space free of clutter.

Take a quick glance at the cover of this book. Chaos is the black web of distraction. Hairy, impulsive, random. White, on the other hand, surrounds the Chaos. And EXECUTE cuts through the Chaos.

So, where do we start?

execute

Think It, Ink It!!

■ **WHAT**

■ **HOW**

■ **WHEN**

Submit your best practices at the link below for the chance to have it featured as a Shot of Octane Video.
https://salesoctane.com/resources/best-practices/

From
to
=

Profession
Professional
SalesPRO

Chapter 3: From Profession to Professional = SalesPRO

Chapter 3

Profession to Professional = SalesPRO

Let's begin with the noun "professional." The word did not exist before 1740. There was "profession," as in one's vocation, but not the word "professional." When the term was first recorded between 1740-1750, it was defined as:

- an expert
- a constant practice
- a learned profession
- for gain

And this person, the Professional, was defined as "A person who earns a living in a occupation frequently engaged in by amateurs." And that, my friends, is the world of sales summed up in one sentence. We are surrounded by amateur salespeople. This is great news! By virtue of reading this book, you have chosen to move in a direction that will separate you from the amateurs. This book is meant to direct you, the salesperson, to the coveted position of Sales Professional or, as we say, the SalesPRO!

Each idea and technique we share in EXECUTE includes a PRO reference because the key to becoming the leader in your space is to become the SalesPRO.

In my last book, *Selling by the BOOK Today: Timeless Wisdom in a Referral Based World*, I took the position that someone in the sales profession must be "good" before they can be great. The book shared the 14 characteristics of being "good" and all of these characteristics are just common sense. The problem is, common sense is no longer common.

Every characteristic to make you "good" in sales was aligned with several PROverbs or PROverbial sayings. It was a wise place to begin the journey. At the time I wrote that book, it never occurred to me there was a PRO in Proverbs. If you commit yourself to instilling the 14 characteristics of "good", this PROverbial wisdom, into your sales process, then it will be easier to EXECUTE and ultimately you will become the SalesPRO. It's just common sense.

But it takes a LOT of EFFORT beginning with the classroom.

execute

Think It, Ink It!!

■ WHAT

■ HOW

■ WHEN

Submit your best practices at the link below for the chance to have it featured as a Shot of Octane Video.
https://salesoctane.com/resources/best-practices/

PROfessor

of Sales

Chapter 4: PROfessor of Sales

Chapter 4

PROfessor of Sales

In 1987, while flipping through the newspaper, I saw an advertisement for a free workshop by the author of Do What You Love the Money Will Follow, Marsha Sinetar. Who would not want to do what they loved? Who would not want money to follow?

It was free, so I went to the session, bought the book following the workshop (it was no longer free), and went home with the intent to do what I loved so I could see the money follow. Within weeks the book was consumed leading to a lifelong pursuit of books. Right now there are another 458 books joining it on the shelf.

Becoming the SalesPRO requires becoming the expert, and becoming the expert requires knowledge. Here's the catch— you are never done, you never arrive. It's not like the pop-up button on a turkey that indicates that you are "done" after a specific amount of time is met.

The "10,000-Hour Rule," shared by Malcolm Gladwell in Outliers[1] has become the solace of many salespeople. If you can just get to 10,000 hours practicing your job you will be the expert! Since the US Government posts average hours worked on a yearly basis as 2,087[2]. Many salespeople believe it's about a five-year run, give or take a few months, and they will be there.

---

[1] Outliers, 2008, Malcolm Gladwell, Little, Brown and Company
[2] https://www.opm.gov/policy-data-oversight/pay-leave/pay-administration/fact-sheets/computing-hourly-rates-of-pay-using-the-2087-hour-divisor/

Even Gladwell suggests in his book that it's more like *ten* years, because you are not always working on your area of expertise. So does everyone arrive as the professional somewhere between 5-10 years in the job?

In his book <u>The Click Moment</u>[3], Frans Johansson suggests the 10,000-Hour Rule for mastery only applies in environments where the rules don't change. The rules have not changed much with playing the guitar, violin or tennis, to use a few of the examples from <u>Outliers</u>. It's just practice, over and over again. Same notes, same ball, same court.

Now look at sales. Look at your industry. Look at the product or service you sell. Look at the different ways in which customers engage with salespeople versus the past. On a scale of 1-10 with 1 being NO CHANGE and 10 being SIGNIFICANT CHANGE, how much change are you experiencing? And this is just at the micro-level of selling.

Next, take a look at the macro-level of knowledge increase because new knowledge drives change. With more knowledge there is more access to knowledge. Watch as your customers grab their mobile device during your sales call and "fact check" your claims.

What does the SalesPRO do in the face of change and the accelerating rate of available knowledge? He/she becomes a Lifelong Learner on the way to becoming the SalesPRO.

The revelation that someone is a Lifelong Learner, however, has become cliché'. The term typically surfaces in a conversation when someone shares they are attending additional-credit college courses during the evenings and weekends. Attending courses is certainly one way to continue your learning. The challenge for the SalesPRO is there are very few college courses on sales. And while any academic pursuit is

---

[3] The Click Moment, 2012, Frans Johansson, Portfolio/Penguin

execute

helpful to learning, it is only one avenue and the SalesPRO has many other resources to use.

So, what and how do you EXECUTE on this skill? What are the habits the SalesPRO creates to become a Lifelong Learner? On the next few pages is a list of where the SalesPRO gains knowledge. It is listed in order of least effort to most effort because you have to start somewhere and oftentimes ease helps to get the process started.

The higher you ascend on the list and the more of the list you cover the greater the probability of becoming and remaining the SalesPRO.

And this list will change as new information and resources become available. We will continue to add information and knowledge on the resources page located on our website at www.salesoctane.com/resources/EXECUTE.

It's called Lifelong for a reason.

1. *Audio Podcasts / Video YouTube clips / Following Social Media threads* – These are typically short hits of knowledge which you can plug in while commuting or when you have a few minutes of time. The key is having a process for capturing any insight you learn. We will cover the process of ways to capture in Chapter 5.

2. *Listen to Books* – Audio books on the topic of sales have become a gold mine for the SalesPRO. The options change frequently so go online and depending on your budget you can go from free to several levels of paid. The key is to use the bookmark options with notes. Define your process to aggregate and implement the knowledge and learning.

3. *Read Books/Hard copy or digital* – Yes, somewhat old school, however, there is something about holding a book (I included this for my wife). The challenge is moving your analog highlights and scribbles on the written page to a digital realm so you can easily retrieve later. Best practice videos on this are available at www.salesoctane.com/resources/EXECUTE.

4. *Read* – Many of you are in industries where there are numerous publications. Many companies put out information for their salespeople regarding trends and other forms of insight. Accumulate them in a pile and when you are waiting somewhere because you are early and the person you are meeting is late you can glance through the pile and rip out what is meaningful. Throw the rest away. It's a great feeling! Define the process for how you aggregate and assimilate the analog information. If you've not picked this up by now, analog is the enemy of EXECUTE.

5. *Listen to attract!* - If you know what kind of knowledge for which you are searching, you will begin to attract conversations that align with your search. What is it you want more knowledge about? The SalesPRO both carries these targets with them and has a process to nurture conversation relative to the targets. The target becomes a magnet for learning from others. One of the PROverbial characteristics of the SalesPRO is seeking wise counsel. The SalesPRO takes advantage of every spontaneous conversation to gain insight.

6. *Courses / Workshops* – Most clients we deal with do some sort of sales training from time to time. This may

execute

include workshops or a course from an academic institution. The challenge is, these courses and workshops can be topical or generic, and it's left to the salesperson to apply the learning to their specific company, product, service or sales process. The SalesPRO goes into every learning environment with their defined visual sales process so they can plug applicable techniques and relevant knowledge right into their unique sales system. For more information on how to create your SalesMap™ go to www.salesoctane.com/resources/EXECUTE.

7. *Mastermind approach* – Assemble a small group to occasionally meet with and discuss a challenge, topic or insight in an effort to leverage the knowledge of others. This group becomes helpful between gatherings when you hit the wall on a particular situation and you need some wise counsel. Mix your group up from time to time. Similar to physical exercise it is helpful to change it up from time to time. Everyone has their angle and it is important to get different angles. Search: *how to create a mastermind group* for great insight on how to create this amazing knowledge resource.

"If you're not prepared to be wrong you'll never come up with anything original"

~ Sir Ken Robinson

8. *Organize your thoughts in writing/text = Journal* - As you begin to implement items 1-7, your brain will begin to explode with new ideas, options, insight and

knowledge. Since you are reading items 1-10 this very minute, and you have yet to begin actually implementing the process, it is essential to stop for moment and think through step 8. One of the challenges associated with lifelong learning is where to go with the knowledge and how you find it later when you need it?

Think about all the sales courses you have taken in the past. Where is all that information? On a shelf, in a 3-ring binder, if you can even find it. It is ANALOG and therein lies the problem. There is no process nor system to find the knowledge when you need it or context of where it should go in your sales process. So, as you accelerate your accumulation of knowledge, you create another problem of knowledge overload.

The journal is a critical link. It must be digital and it must become a habit. New options surface on a regular basis. For a current list of options go to www.salesoctane.com/resources/EXECUTE.

9. *Write original content: small - medium – Tweet/Blog/Article* - Write about the space you are in. Start very small. Perhaps the size of a tweet. Start with a few sentences. Literally, take your relevant ideas and organize your thoughts to 140 characters (roughly 28 words). Once you have a few sentences (tweets) you can expand the writing to create a blog or post in your area of influence. If you reference other articles and knowledge sources simply include a link to the material and you become generous, a key characteristic of being "good." Then, when others like or follow your media or industry posts, you know you are onto something which will boost your confidence to continue learning.

execute

My guess is you are thinking "I have ZERO time for this and I don't like to write..." This is the end goal and it will take time—perhaps quarters or even years—to get there, but you *will* get there!

10. *Share/Speak/Present/Write an Article/Book* – Go big. You know you have arrived, **for the moment***, when others ask you to share your insight to a broad audience. The teacher often learns more than the student because the teacher must prepare to teach. In the process of preparing you become wiser and more proficient with the knowledge.

> *"The toughest thing about success is that you've got to keep on being a success."*
>
> *~ Irving Berlin*

***"...for the moment"** Expect your energy for learning to grow once you implement these best practices. Success breeds success and knowledge creates desire for more knowledge. This is important since the knowledge will change and we are only as good as our current knowledge, hence Lifelong Learner. My guess is this is why Marsha Sinetar began the title of the book with "do what you love" because this makes learning a lot easier.

Become the SalesPRO by becoming the PROfessor of Sales!

Jim Ryerson

Think It, Ink It!!

■ **WHAT**

■ **HOW**

■ **WHEN**

Submit your best practices at the link below for the chance to have it featured as a Shot of Octane Video.
https://salesoctane.com/resources/best-practices/

PROgram —
of

The Power
1

Chapter 5: PROgram – The Power of 1

Chapter 5

PROgram – The Power of 1

Who's in control of your life? Not on a spiritual level—that's a different conversation. On a purely sales level, how do you look at the incoming and outgoing information that constantly hits you on a daily basis? Who's in control? There's a body of research that suggests those who see themselves as being in control achieve greater success than those who believe others are in control[4].

It's referred to as your locus of control. Locus simply means your position or place of control. The question is do you see yourself as being in control or do you see others controlling you. The SalesPRO takes accountability and enters every day and situation with the mindset they are in control. So what do you do when you feel like you are OUT of control?

Several years ago, a friend of mine made the recommendation to "control the controllables," and I've never forgotten their words. But what does it mean for the SalesPRO to control the controllables?

Salespeople live in a world of chaos. Much of the chaos is incoming. Incoming calls, email, text, notifications, reminders, CRM tasks, requests, inquiries, questions and a host of other sources. These are typically from customers who are growing increasingly impatient[5] with what often borders on unrealistic

---

[4] http://wilderdom.com/psychology/loc/LocusOfControlWhatIs.html
[5] http://www.pewinternet.org/2012/02/29/millennials-will-benefit-and-suffer-due-to-their-hyperconnected-lives-2/

expectations. The chaos could also be coming from your team or superiors. Or, of course, from your personal life. Here's the thing. You cannot control what others do. Aside from misguided attempts involving manipulation, there is virtually nothing you can do to control what other people do. So, by definition, these are uncontrollable. All we can do is react and action beats reaction.

We'll get back to what to do with "others" later but for now let's focus on the actions the SalesPRO takes to be in control.

1 Place

In 1955, Dr. Cyril Northcote Parkinson coined what is referred to as Parkinson's Law: "Work expands so as to fill the time available for its completion." Parkinson's Law applies to everything from time management to government budgets and everything in between.

An easy way to visualize this concept is to think of those self-storage facilities and their incredible growth in popularity. Once you have one, you simply keep acquiring items to fill it, until you need a larger one. If you have the space, you will fill it…good or bad.

The same theory applies to your information, notes, reminders, files, knowledge, and everything else you accumulate. The more places you stash this accumulation, the more places you will generate. Then you have to find it, and guess what? It's like having 100 storage doors, all orange, and you can't remember which one holds the article you are looking for. Chaos ensues. If we don't cut through the minutia, it will cut through us in the form of lower productivity and a lack of focus.

While Artificial Intelligence, AI, will continue to improve our ability to locate items (think Spotlight in iOS), this only works relative to the area being searched. So, limit the area and you will limit the search time.

execute

How? Personally (and as a team), evaluate every place content, including knowledge, accumulates, and begin to consolidate until you have ONE PLACE.

☐ **1 List**

Writing things down on paper, sticky notes or dictating them into our digital devices is critical. The challenge becomes, we now have a sea of sticky notes, notepads, journals, and several apps, all of which accumulate a list of what we need to do. The lists become overwhelming. We often seek the solace in the easiest item we can find, so we can complete it and feel good about our progress. The result is, we exchange the most important and oftentimes challenging action for the least-urgent, least-challenging action and we feel good... for the moment.

Why do we resist putting everything into one list? Simple, it is overwhelming when you look at the list. This effort will follow Kanter's Law.)

"Everything looks like a failure in the middle"

– Rosabeth Moss Kanter

It's messy in the middle. It will start out positive since the process of gathering everything into one place is not difficult and will make you feel like you are making some significant progress. Then it gets very messy. The list is so long it creates anxiety. The list is real and you own it because you committed to it so keep moving.

As you move through the process you will realize many of the items on the list are the result of significant over-commitments, unqualified opportunities, unrealistic expectations and poor choices. This process begins to train you to manage your commitments, qualify opportunities earlier in the sales cycle, manage your and other's expectations and make better choices. It's messy in the middle. Eventually you EXECUTE on the right activities more greater frequency. (JIM... read the previous sentence outloud... I have no idea what it means!)The SalesPRO consolidates their list in ONE PLACE making it easier to prioritize and EXECUTE.

EXECUTE Bonus: Once your list is in digital notes (see 1 and done), you only see the list when you want to! This reduces your anxiety and allows you to focus on the task at hand.

☐ **1 Way out of the brain**

In chapter 2, we referred to the clear uncluttered area of the brain scan as White Space. White is the absence of color, so it's like White Space is the absence of clutter in your brain. The more we keep trying to think of things to remember, and attempting to hold them in our memory, the more clutter begins to build. And the more clutter, the less white space. This is the easiest of all the steps the SalesPRO will take in this book:

When you think it, ink it!

Who uses ink anymore? The reason for the use of the word ink is so the phrase rhymes, and rhymes are easier to remember[6].

The SalesPRO gets ideas, reminders, random to-do's, and insight out of their brain and into a digital form so it can be easily

---

[6] https://web.stanford.edu/~gbower/1969/why_rhymes_easy_learn.pdf

retrieved at a time when it is needed. This removes much of the clutter in the brain and creates the white space necessary to EXECUTE.

How – During the day (or at night if you live alone) whether in the car, office, walking, exercising or just hanging out - Embrace voice to text technology. Learn how to navigate one voice to text app to dictate your thoughts quickly and get them out of your brain. Because it's digital, you can efficiently move it to its best location for the next step. Also, because it is digital, it is easily searchable so you can find it later.

This is the difference between digital, which is a dynamic medium, versus analog, which is static—think handwriting on paper. Oddly enough, the opposite of dynamic is unproductive and ineffective. A key to EXECUTE is dynamic digital capture of all your thoughts in one place so you can become productive and effective.

While in front of others (think customer facing) – Write it down in the moment because:

- a. This demonstrates to the other person that what they are saying is so important you want to capture it right away. You can bolster their self-esteem and their confidence in you as a salesperson, all while helping yourself create white space in your brain. Win-win!
- b. It keeps you from talking too much. When you are writing, it is difficult to also talk up a storm. The less you talk, the more they will talk—and you learn very little while you are talking.
- c. Comprehensive notes make it much easier to organize the follow-up confirmation of the conversation.
- d. Depending on your sales cycle, you may have multiple conversations. Having copious notes of each interaction makes the process much easier for you and

your team members. Your notes improve your memory of the conversation the next time you revisit the situation.

At night –Have you ever noticed how often you think of a new idea or something you need to remember while falling asleep? The fact is we often think of ideas and ruminate on them as we doze off or even as we wake. And of course, as we "are carried along the river of dreams" (apologies to Billy Joel), we continue to dwell on the issues of our waking life.

Regardless of when these ideas surface during your sleep cycle, the key is to get it out of your brain so you know with confidence you will have it when you need it. Simply having ONE PLACE to write on and write with next to your bed solves this problem. Avoid your digital device as it annoys others in the room and if you stare at the screen you will disrupt a great night of sleep!

One of our daughters is a funeral director who receives challenging calls in the middle of the night, usually from someone who is dealing with the most difficult of moments. Early on, she developed a checklist of questions to ask the caller so she not only provides the best user experience to someone who is facing a terrible situation, but also she knows with confidence that she has all the information and will not need to call back several times. She keeps the checklist and a pen next to the bed every evening before she turns the light out.

Between ONE APP on ONE MOBILE device and ONE DIGITAL NOTEBOOK (see 1 and Done), and the occasional nighttime piece of paper you should have all you need to digitally capture your thoughts in a form you can easily retrieve later.

This begins to create some white space in your brain so you can finally think!

EXECUTE BONUS: Once you move a thought to text, whether written or dictated digitally, it is out of your mind. It becomes far easier to share your ideas with others.

"Get it from here

to there

and it is easier to share."

– Jim Ryerson

☐ **1 Calendar**

The leather-bound calendar was a common gift from many a salesperson to their customer—with the company logo emblazoned on the front as a constant reminder to buy their product or use their service. The better the calendar, the greater the probability they would use your gift heading into the New

Jim Ryerson

Year. Those calendars which came in second place (or worse) were brought home to family members, or cascaded down to others in the office. At home was a family calendar for your personal life and then you had your leather-bound business calendar for your professional life.

The Daytimer took it to a whole other level, but again you had your personal calendar at home and your Daytimer for work. Then came the PDA – Personal Digital Assistant, and finally in 2007, we completely gave up our ability to separate our personal and professional lives. 2007 brought the first iOS phone and Android followed close behind. While there are still some paper holdouts, each subsequent generation will become less attached to the paper calendar or leather-bound notebook calendar. R.I.P.

For the SalesPRO the calendar built into their CRM is also THEIR calendar.

☐ 1 CRM – Customer Relationship Management platform

Because information is power, the SalesPRO embraces CRM. Every contact, every prospect, every customer, every meeting, every email, everything goes into CRM so you and your company can data-mine trends. Your CRM becomes the backbone of your Digital and even Analog (think snail mail) marketing. Your CRM is the vault of information used for AI. Without a dedicated CRM you are unable to use everything coming down the path for SEO, SEM, PPC, AI and every other digital acronym.

CRM had a bad reputation right out of the gate due to over-controlling Managers. Management often used CRM exclusively to track activity and punish salespeople who were not hitting

execute

certain activity metrics. This was often even when the salesperson was exceeding quota.

Most of this abuse is gone and companies have settled into using CRM to drive the marketing and sales process. The order of the last sentence, marketing before sales process, is intentional. The contact names and emails are often mined by Marketing for their outbound marketing efforts. However, driving the sales process will help the salesperson and that must be the intent of CRM. If CRM does not help you improve the efficiency and effectiveness of your work, it will not be embraced and it will eventually die. Yes, your CRM will RIP. Lose-Lose. One key to CRM is the next step, which we cover in Chapter 6.

☐ **1 And done – digital notebooks**

One of the easiest habits to modify is the move from handwritten notes on paper to digital "handwritten" notes. Years ago, on a flight, I had the good fortune to sit next to a PhD who shared with me his insight on habit formation. He mentioned one of the keys to learning a new habit is unlearning the old habit. Then he made the statement, "The best new habits are the ones which require minor shifts to get the desired result." This makes sense. So why resist the easy move to digital handwritten notes?

You are sitting in front of your customer asking questions and your customer is sharing key information. You begin writing on the pad of paper or journal you use for notes. When you are done, you go to your next appointment and continue on the same/new page with the next conversation. Between appointments, you get three calls and add those notes between the appointment notes. Along the way you randomly think of 5-7 personal items you need to deal with and write those on the same page so you won't forget them. Before long you have several

Jim Ryerson

pages of notes with multiple entries which belong in multiple places.

Think about it this way: what you are basically doing with handwritten notes is putting all your conversations into one word document day after day. That would be nuts. This is why you have multiple folders for different clients, projects and situations, and then within those folders you have multiple documents. This makes it much easier to find later and reduces the chaos you would have if you put everything in one document. What is different with handwritten notes?

Once you move to digital notes, you can begin each different conversation with its own unique digital notebook page. At the end of the day or meeting, you can copy, paste and move your handwritten notes between documents and into the relevant folders. Retrieval of the last conversation is one click away. Because it is digital it is searchable. Even though it is handwritten, the APPs transcribe your handwriting to text, and once it is text, it is searchable. If that's not all...you literally carry every note you ever wrote with you all the time. And it's backed up to the cloud, so team members can see your notes.

EXECUTE Bonus if you are easily distracted you may find the tactile nature of writing digitally is like therapy for your brain.

☐ **1 Way to start and finish**

We know anecdotally that when we take time to plan a task before we throw ourselves into that task, we save time in the long run. What is different about each day? We tend to check email, text, voicemail and our calendar and begin to react to what is thrown our way. Chaos ensues.

execute

There is only one way to start the day. After a few minutes or more of getting yourself centered for the day *then* have a quick look at your world, identify your priorities and then begin to EXECUTE. It's a great way to start the day! Right now on average it takes me approximately 45 minutes to "start the day" right.

The process is no different at the end of the day. Before you close it down ,run through the same checklist to clean up what needs to move forward to a later date, perhaps tomorrow, and say to yourself "we're done for the day!" It's a great way to leave the work behind and truly end the workday! Right now I average 60 minutes to "end the day" which means I often think about when I need to leave the office or stop working and begin my end the day process one hour before. This is not easy, however, it becomes easier over time.

How? The system will change as you add more places where projects and information reside. Hence the power of 1. Details on how to Start the Day / End the Day are found in Chapter 8 PROactive.

☐ 1 system/platform/app

This is a fast one, however it is critical so it must be addressed. Too often salespeople use more than one system or platform or app versus standardizing. Worse, companies allow salespeople to use whatever they wish versus coming up with a single solution and leveraging the best practices of the user groups.

We've all been there when someone shows us an application they are using. We get excited and plan to use it ourselves. In most cases you must have been using something to accomplish the same result before. The question is, did you go all-in on the new approach or are you now using both? Before

Jim Ryerson

long we have multiple ways of accomplishing a similar result. Now multiply this by the entire sales team and you can see the challenge. Every team member is spending time learning the details of the new approach and in most cases they abandon it for the next new approach. The SalesPRO evaluates new platforms, systems and applications with the input of their team and/or other SalesPRO users. They make a decision to move to the new system/platform/app and burn the ships with the old solution. All in.

NOTE: There is no "best" solution which lasts forever. New Systems/Platforms/Apps are a fact of life, which is another reason why the SalesPRO is a lifelong learner!

At this point in the POWER OF 1, you may be asking yourself, "Where does this end?" Good question. Because new technology will provide new ways to improve efficiency through alignment and consolidation, the answer is never. It never ends, which is why we need to embrace learning new applications and align with the best ONE for us.

> *"Rome was not built in 1 day"*
>
> *– John Heywood*

The key in each of these options to consolidate to one solution is to take them one at a time, and then be open to additional consolidation as new technologies surface.

☐ 1 Everything – UNLESS

There is one exception to the Power of 1. A few years back I had my wireless presentation device seize up. The key was stuck and it was not repairable. There was no backup, and it became a torturous day. I now carry two duplicate presentation devices because it is a deal-breaker if one fails during a workshop or presentation. I've heard of some executives who carry two mirrored laptops in case one fails. So, there are, in fact, a few duplicates and they are the exception and not the rule. The more you have the more you have to deal with. Leverage the Power of 1 and watch the white space grow!

Think It, Ink It!!

■ WHAT

■ HOW

■ WHEN

Submit your best practices at the link below for the chance to have it featured as a Shot of Octane Video.
https://salesoctane.com/resources/best-practices/

A PRO
in

is Found
PROcess

Chapter 6: A PRO is Found in PROcess

Chapter 6

A PRO is Found in PROcess

The word PROcess aligns with PROcedures, rules and measurements. "Process" is typically reserved for the structured, obedient, submissive, and law-abiding of the world, which is one of the reasons some may be inclined to skip over this chapter. Please don't. The SalesPRO embraces PROcess, as it is the antidote to many of the challenges they face as a direct result of their natural behavioral style.

"You can control your behavior but you cannot control the consequences"

- Anon

The consequences of not following a PROcess are dire. It often begins as an over-commitment here or there. This begins to look like a failure to deliver. Missed dates become a poor User eXperience and before long we cannot be trusted.

You simply cannot drop the ball anymore when selling or implementing a sale because with reviews, recommendations and social media you will be known. And because it takes more touches to finally talk with and get in front of a prospect, this constant juggling to stay on top of your next step becomes challenging at best. At its worst, we fail to follow up and ultimately lose track of the opportunity.

The good news is your CRM can drive your sales process, eliminate a forgotten task and reduce your chaos. Every activity you take off-line from your CRM is at risk and will ultimately create more chaos.

If you believe you or your company is not taking full advantage of the sales process improvements with CRM then here are some helpful tips.

   a. Map out your sales process step by laborious step. If your company has a 5, 6, 10, or even 20-Step process, you should be suspicious. You can't build out a sales CRM with a high-level view of sales. When we ask the question, "Do you have a defined sales process?", we often hear clients respond with their "6 step" process: Lead, Prospect, Qualify, Appointment, Propose, Close… or some variation on this theme. Your CRM won't be able to help you if that's your process. That's how you measure a sales funnel to get a forecast and that's why most CRM's feel like punishment. Over the years of doing sales-mapping at Sales Octane we have never had a client with less than 40 steps in the most basic sales process, once we are finished exhausting the reality of what the salespeople do (or should be doing). Driving the sales process and helping the salesperson requires identifying every step in the process and automating the reminders.

   b. Incorporate all the reminders of each next step into the CRM and automate each next step. Why? Because much of what you struggle with is keeping track of all the activities and next steps of a growing list of targets/suspects, prospects, customers and accounts. It is becoming more of a challenge as more influencers

execute

are involved in the decision from the customer side *and* those contacts change roles within or moves from one company to another. Nothing has changed from our predictions and research in *Selling by the BOOK Today*. The only way to create white space in your brain is to embrace your CRM and gain confidence it has all the information you need *including the next activity in the sales process* in one place.

GIGO is a computer-science acronym for "Garbage In, Garbage Out." The same goes for CRM. If you fail to enter the information accurately, then all CRM will do is increase the velocity of your chaos. Often referred to as Process Builder in many CRM packages, the time-saver for the SalesPRO is when their CRM allows them to initiate a key step— such as a new lead/target, proposal, closed sale, or referral—and by entering a few details, the CRM auto-populates all of the reminders and next steps so the SalesPRO can EXECUTE!

c. As you use your CRM, keep track of when you drop the ball. When you catch yourself saying, "I should have done this, or that," then go back to the CRM and see if there is a way to incorporate an automated reminder in your CRM. Whenever you say, "Did I remember to," or, "I have to remember to," then go back to the CRM and see if there is a way to incorporate an automated reminder. The white space in your brain occurs when you can say with confidence "forget about it…it's in CRM and CRM will remind me later…guaranteed."

d. Share CRM best practices with your team, including micro-learning screen-capture videos, to help you implement the best practices. Whoever is your Sales PROcess holder must have routine check-ins using a Broke/Unclear/Best Practice approach. Ask yourself and the team:

Broke
"What is broken in our current PROcess?" When you Think It, Ink It. Don't just talk about it, write it down. In some cases, it's not broken but rather it is not being used or executed properly. So, share how to do it correctly and the process improves. Anything still on the list can be prioritized and improved! Keep the list going since if you personally have a need there are another million salespeople out there with the same problem and a wise CRM provider will come up with a fix or feature before long!

Unclear
"What is unclear in our current PROcess?" When you Think It, Ink It. Don't just talk about it, write it down. If your current team is unclear about certain processes in your CRM then you can bet there will be similar questions as new team members come on board. Once you have it defined, you can clarify, and the process improves.

Best Practice
"What are your best practices in our current PROcess?" Salespeople often have great ideas on work-arounds within the system, or they have best practices from their former employers. Some ideas may require modifying your CRM, so add it to the list, share it with your CRM provider and everything improves!

execute

"The system works when you work in the system"

– Jim Ryerson

Last step and this is *critical*. In Chapter 13, PROgress vs. Perfection, we run through an exercise on how to create short screen-share videos showing each function or best practice with any technology. When you EXECUTE this best practice you create a library of short screen-share videos that the SalesPRO can pull up alongside their CRM and become the lifelong learner.

Much of CRM success is simply learning. Learning takes practice and practice means mistakes and frustration. It's part of the process of becoming the SalesPRO and it is a never-ending process.

Here's the payoff:

- 👍 *Leads* – your Digital Marketing team relies on your database of contacts and information in CRM. More names, contact information and data lead to more leads.
- 👍 *Connections* – your ability to find a personal or business connection increases exponentially with a robust CRM.
- 👍 *AI* – as Artificial Intelligence gains acceptance, much of the information it will intelligently evaluate will be your CRM. So, no information = little intelligence.
- 👍 *Clear mind/less chaos* – CRM gives you the confidence you will not forget anything, ever. If it's in CRM, it is in the digital bank!

👍 *Management* – The next time someone on the leadership team asks you for a progress update, just send him or her to your CRM. As the leadership team sees the accuracy of the CRM, which drives the forecast/funnel, they will interrupt less and allow you to EXECUTE.

👍 *Freedom* – What often looks like restriction is actually meant to keep us out of trouble. Once you have your CRM supporting your sales activity, it will free you up to do more of what you love—sell.

👍 *More selling time* – As you fine-tune your CRM, it will allow you to spend more time selling and less time updating. CRM is technology and it will keep improving. Trust the CRM. Trust the PROcess!

execute

Think It, Ink It!!

■ WHAT

■ HOW

■ WHEN

Submit your best practices at the link below for the chance to have it featured as a Shot of Octane Video.
https://salesoctane.com/resources/best-practices/

PROmise = YES be

Let Your YES

Chapter 7: PROmise = Let Your YES be YES

Chapter 7

PROmise = Let Your YES be YES

As you begin to EXECUTE the "One Place" strategy and live in CRM, you may begin to experience challenges with time management. This is because you can finally view all your commitments and work to be done in one place. Now we move to the next step, which is gaining control of your commitments— or what may be over-commitments.

Ask yourself the question, "What do I fear?" This question often gets to the core of many of our struggles as a salesperson. When it comes to challenges and problems we face on a daily basis, we often spend our time at the level of the symptom. Some of these symptoms include not enough time, too many commitments, lack of priorities, easily distracted, etc.

Then we jump to the quick fix of working nights and weekends, getting more overcommitted, racing between what is urgently at hand, buying yet another productivity/organization APP which we fail to implement and overall just working harder. In the end we feel overcommitted and chaotic. Living on the symptom level will never resolve the actual challenge.

So, "What do you fear?" If you were working with an organizational psychologist, they would keep scratching at your answer until you arrive at the root cause. This might be failure in a job (no sales, lost sales, not hitting your sales goal, etc.), failure in a relationship (disappointing your manager, prospect, customer, team, family, etc.), or failure to self (not capable, not worthy, someone will figure me out). So, what is it?

Why we do what we do is critically important at this phase in building a foundation to EXECUTE.

> *"If I only had 1 hour to solve a problem, I would spend 55 minutes defining the problem and the remaining 5 minutes solving it"*[7]
>
> –Anon

Variations of this quote, often misattributed to Einstein, Dewey or Charles Kettering, do make sense. It's common sense. Before running off without a plan, it is best to figure out what the problem is first and putting a plan together. This is what your clients are looking for when they agree to meet with you. They would prefer you understand their situation and help them clearly diagnose their problem before you offer solutions. The SalesPRO diagnoses before they prescribe. They are like Sales Doctors. So, take the same approach with properly diagnosing why you have the problem of chaos.

We are not suggesting you spend your entire day defining your problems. We are suggesting you spend some time right now getting to the root of your chaos so you can build a system to EXECUTE. You may find the root of your challenges comes from your greatest strength, your people orientation and your optimism. Leverage your strength and adapt in challenge. This is the mantra of the SalesPRO, and it requires a clear understanding and definition of both your strengths and your challenges.

Recall the reference in Chapter 2 to the results of the assessment of salespeople since our start in 2003. Right off the bat, we noticed a pattern emerging with the assessment results from the salespeople coming through our programs. The largest

---

[7] https://quoteinvestigator.com/2014/05/22/solve/

execute

percentage of salespeople—a disproportionate amount—was extroverted versus introverted. This makes sense. Hire salespeople who get their energy from being around other people because we want them to generate new relationships.

The second insight was that a disproportionate percentage of salespeople were people-oriented and cooperative vs. task and detail oriented. This also makes sense. Hire salespeople who are people-oriented so they can draw customers and prospects alike. So, what's the problem?

Before we get to the problem, it is important we take a few minutes to reinforce the fact that being Extroverted and/or People-oriented is a very positive trait and will get you in front of more people. You are networking machines. You build a web of connections that gets you in front of new prospects and those who influence your customers. Everyone invites you to events because you are often the life of the event. You are a giver! You volunteer for association and charity events and you are at the center of everything.

This is a gift that many people wish they had. So, use it! We reinforce in *First 100 Days of Selling, First 100 Days of In-home Selling* and *Selling by the BOOK Today* that these behavioral characteristics are to be celebrated and leveraged. So, leverage them. And define how, when and where they can become a problem.

Question: What is the problem? Answer: Over-commitment!

We make promises every day. When we commit to call someone, arrive at an appointment, send the proposal, follow up, or hand in our forecast. Just fill in the blank of the items on your task list. Your to-dos. How many of those to-dos are you behind on? How many of the items are others, including your team, chasing you down for? When you look at the list, how does it make you feel? Overcommitted, stressed, anxious and looking for a way out?

The way out begins with the way in.

How do we get ourselves into each of these situations in the first place? While a few of them are imposed upon us, the forecast for instance, the remainder are self-imposed.

Look down at your to-do list, your task list on CRM and your calendar for the next 30 days. How many of these items did you commit to without asking the other person when they needed it completed? How many of your commitments did you confirm the customer's next step once you sent them the information? How many of these commitments or appointments are qualified opportunities? How do you know? Or, did the fear of being disliked and rejected cause your "pleasing tendency" to overcommit?

Remember, in the short term your strategy of overcommitting works. It really does! The other person responds with a positive affirmation. You feel liked. Zero rejection. The probability of a sale feels certain! And the list of over-commitments just grew. The chaos continues.

In their book <u>What you Fear is Who you Are</u>, Dr. David Thompson and Krysten Thompson explore the correlation between fear and how it drives our decisions. One of my early mentors, Robal Johnson, a personal friend of Dr. Thompson, used this information to help me diagnose where and how I needed to adapt in order to EXECUTE at a higher level. While neither he nor I knew it at the time this correlation of fear and failed events is essential in order for many salespeople to EXECUTE on a daily basis.

Take a look at your behavioral style. What is it? Introverted, Extroverted, more People-oriented or Task/Detail oriented? Until

execute

you know it is very difficult to leverage your strengths and diagnose your challenges. Without the diagnosis you have only anecdotal evidence.

Take a look at your task list and ask yourself the question, "How do I get into these situations?" What you may find is a lot of the tasks are a result of over-commitments you have made or others have placed on you.

> *"A lack of planning on your part does not constitute an emergency on my part"*
>
> *- Anon*

> *"Unless, of course, it is your customer or leader"*
>
> *–Jim Ryerson*

Many of the over-commitments on your task list and calendar are the result of the unrealistic expectations of customers or leaders. This is not going to change, as we discussed in *Selling by the BOOK Today*. If anything, the unrealistic requests will increase. The key is how you respond up front when the request is made. This goes back to controlling the controllables in Chapter 5. When you take control of incoming requests you have a greater probability of managing the expectations of both customers and leadership and reducing your chaos. It's a win-win.

First, always slow the process down and think before you reply. Second, the following two questions will help to gather additional information from the requestor in an effort to both buy you some much-needed time to think and often elicits a response from the requestor which is beneficial to you (as in more time to complete the task, more information on the next step and a host of other helpful insights). So practice these and keep them at the ready.

When do you need it?
Once I get it to you, what's the/your next step?

Both are open-ended questions prompting the requestor to at least think about what they are asking you for. While they are thinking, you have additional brain time to process how best to handle their request. Have confidence in your ability to evaluate requests and manage their expectations and your commitments. While this will not resolve every situation it will begin to reduce over-commitments by aligning the commitment with the need.

Second, many of the over-commitments you have on your calendar and list are related to unqualified opportunities. You are over-committed with tasks associated with an opportunity which you have little or no probability of winning. Worse, while there is no research to confirm this, most salespeople will tell you that unqualified, long shot opportunities take far more time than qualified higher probability sale. This is one of the reasons the SalesPRO exhausts every opportunity to increase share of wallet within existing clients where it is much easier to qualify.

Again, go back to the calendar and task list and identify where you are spending your time. Managing expectations and qualifying opportunities is far more challenging especially when you are new to sales or behind quota. Both situations literally attract over commitments and the pursuit of unqualified opportunities.

execute

Once you begin the process of pursuing unqualified opportunities in an effort to be liked, you pretty much ensure you will be disliked.

Think about it. You over-commit to be liked because you have a fear of failure, fear of being disliked or fear of rejection. The next thing you know you have over-committed.

Now you either:

- ☹ fail to meet the over-commitment you made = and you become disliked by the person you failed.
- ☹ work long hours, nights and weekends to meet the over-commitment you made = and you become disliked by those who had planned to spend quality time with you.
- ☹ force others on your team to work long hours, nights and weekends to meet the over-commitments you made = you don't even want to know what they think when they see you coming. Once again you become disliked.

Now, add to this little mess the reality that the over-commitment was for an unqualified opportunity, so you lose the deal. You get the very thing you set out to avoid—another failed event.

Ultimately, you will become exactly what you fear *unless* you understand what is driving your PROmise to yourself and others. Over-commitments driven by fear are self-inflicted and a major cause of our chaos. Building a PROmise based on a PROactive plan is the start of improvement!

Jim Ryerson

Think It, Ink It!!

■ **WHAT**

■ **HOW**

■ **WHEN**

Submit your best practices at the link below for the chance to have it featured as a Shot of Octane Video.
https://salesoctane.com/resources/best-practices/

The

is

SalesPRO PROactive

Chapter 8: The SalesPRO is PROactive

Chapter 8

The SalesPRO is PROactive

If there was ever made a movie titled "The Day in the Life of a Salesperson," it would definitely be an action-packed thrill ride. The action figure would be the salesperson and they would be moving all day long, executing conversations, paperwork, email, text, taking calls, making calls and brief meetings and conversations with their team members. Salespeople are executing all day long! The question is whether this is really action or reaction? As we discussed at the start of Chapter 5, action beats reaction. To make sure your actions throughout the day are not just a series of *reactions* requires the word PROactive. The SalesPRO spends more of their time in PROactive work that positions them for the right type of action.

In his 1989 book <u>The Practical Guide to Joint Ventures and Corporate Alliances</u>, Robert Porter Lynch shared that Einstein was once asked how he would spend his time if he was given a problem upon which his life depended and he had only one hour to solve it. Einstein responded by saying he would spend 30 minutes analyzing the problem, 20 minutes planning the solution, and ten minutes executing the solution.

The exact ratio of analysis, planning and executing is not important. What is critical is there are two steps prior to EXECUTE: analysis and planning. Salespeople are born action figures. When you surround yourself with a system to help you analyze and formulate your actions, you will EXECUTE a plan of action and reduce reactions.

Jim Ryerson

While every client is different because of their sales process and business model, we have found three consistent points where a PROactive step is critical so start here:

- The start of your day
- Every significant Prospect/Customer/Client/Sales engagement
- Account Strategy

You may have other watershed moments in your sale where PROactive thinking and planning is essential. This will simply provide the reason why along with the what, how and when for the three we've noted above.

Why: Would'a, Should'a, Could'a

Think about your most recent appointment where you realized you had forgotten to bring, prepare or have something you wish you had taken along? We know that 80% of our sales calls follow a similar flow, so why don't we have everything with us or prepared in advance?

How often do you get off the phone with a prospect, sign off a screen-share appointment with a customer, or walk out of a client presentation and wish you had made a few changes in your approach? Or you wish you had a question, a statement, a response to an objection, or even a challenge to their position? It happens all the time. We know we should capture these modifications and incorporate them into future sales calls. And then we are on to the next call, so we commit to remember for next time.

How often do you share the outcome of a sales call with a team member or your leader upon your return and they offer

execute

several ideas that would have helped had you thought about them before the call? We know our sales strategy improves when we solicit the insight of others, However, we never seem to have time for these proactive conversations.

When was the last time your leader asked you for the next step with a prospect and your response was, "I need to follow up on that!" *There's a confidence builder for your leader.* Walking out of every sales engagement, we know we should always have a next step confirmed. But it always seems like the end of the call comes suddenly and the only thing you can think to say is, "This has been great …I will follow up in a couple of weeks." Hmmm. The prospect even smiled as you walked out the door.

When was the last time you had a dead-end prospecting call, only to find out later during a spontaneous conversation with someone in your company that they know a key influencer at the account? The challenge is, you took your best shot and now it's too late. We know there is benefit in gaining the connections, relationships, knowledge and experience of others. But there's no efficient way to gather that information other than an email blast to the company and most find those annoying.

Knowing why you need to become more PROactive is not the issue. You know why as soon as you answer those questions. You know why every time you wish you had been better prepared. Here's the catch. *Why* seldom resolves anything. It is critical to know why…however, the key to improving is found in the words *what, how* and *when*. So, what should you do differently, how should you make this proactive approach become your new routine, and when? When should you EXECUTE on each new routine? When will you start?

Jim Ryerson

What? The PROactive way to start and end your day.

"It's difficult to recover from a bad start"

– Jim Ryerson

If you ever watch a track and field race, you will notice each runner has a very consistent pre-race ritual. They don't do *random*. Some of the rituals are superstitious: the lucky shoes or shirt, eating the same thing before each race, avoiding eye contact, etc. Many of the rituals are routines that can improve the outcome: stretching, self-talk, a specific way they put on their socks, etc. My favorite story came from Coach John Wooden, who would "take the entire first squad meeting, held two weeks before the initial practice, to personally demonstrate exactly how to put on a sock. This painstakingly detailed demonstration was important because any small fold or wrinkle in a sock, no matter how minor, could lead to blisters which would have a negative impact on their performance." (Wooden, Coach John Wooden with Steve Jamison, pg 60 Details Create Success 1997 McGraw Hill)

"You never have to recover from a good start"

– Bobby Davis

Why should the SalesPRO be any different? This is even more critical if you begin or spend your day in an office with interruptions and distractions. By having a consistent routine of how you look at and then plan your day, you can maintain a

execute

clearer focus on what needs to get done. This allows you to begin to EXECUTE right away. The best part is this is something you personally control... so take control of your day right at the start!

WHAT – We refer to this as our "Kickstart the Day" approach because it is intended to kick you into gear. Exactly what is included on your Kickstart the day list depends on your situation and your routine. As your situation changes you may find it necessary to modify the checklist. Below is an example:

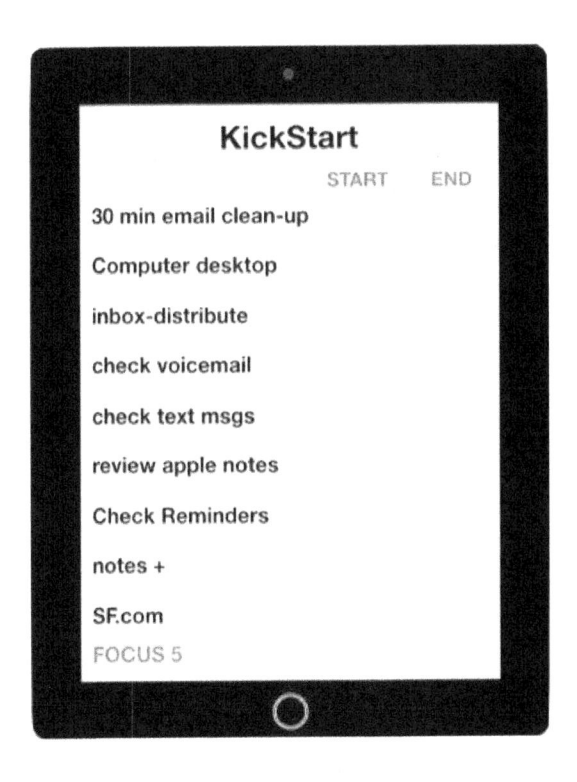

KickStart

START   END

30 min email clean-up

Computer desktop

inbox-distribute

check voicemail

check text msgs

review apple notes

Check Reminders

notes +

SF.com

FOCUS 5

Take a look at all the places where requests, tasks, projects and clutter accumulates. In my case, as I'm writing this book, I have it down to nine buckets. I can look at my email, computer desktop, inbox (my physical inbox), voicemail, text messages, Apple notes, Apple reminders, my Notes Plus (digital handwriting notebook, your version of yellow lined pads or fashionable journals), and finally my CRM (Salesforce), which is also my calendar.

You may be wondering why I don't have everything in one place given the fact we discussed the idea of ONE PLACE in chapter 5. My guess, however, is you will find that you have far more than nine. Those piles of paper on your desk...add a bucket called PILES ON DESK. If you like sticky notes...add a bucket called STICKY NOTES. If your company has a project-tracking APP, add this bucket to your list. Hear me now...nine is pretty good. It took me several months to get it down to nine.

Of course, it is possible something may be developed tomorrow which will consolidate two of more of these buckets into one, and then I will celebrate the consolidation. For now, this is my world. So, take a look at your world and write down the high-level buckets where new requests, tasks, projects and clutter tends to accumulate. This may be overwhelming. Remember, it often gets worse before it gets better.

In some cases, you may have buckets that will pull you in and trap you for way too long. In those cases, it helps to add a maximum time you will spend on those buckets, similar to my current "30 Minutes E-mail." I know I will personally never handle all my email in one sitting. I have accepted that. So, I triage my email first thing in the morning and I've selected 30 minutes as my number. So, literally set a timer and don't allow yourself to spend any more time on whatever you have gotten pulled into in the past. In most cases I can triage email in less than 30 minutes, which gives me a reward!

HOW – Review the checklist at the start of each day. When you finish looking at your world, then create a list of what you need to do to count today a success. We call this the "Focus 5," and you can watch the video on Shot Of Octane® Mobile APP. They key is to only have 5 to-dos in front of you at a time. More becomes overwhelming. You can't do it all, so select the 5 most important, prioritize them and EXECUTE!

EXECUTE Bonus: The first few days you complete this process you may recognize you are over-committed. Review Chapter 7.

WHEN – Kickstart your day at the start of your day or the tendency is to start completing low priority tasks to "feel good." Occasionally someone will suggest doing this the night before. This may adversely affect your sleep as we discuss in Chapter 12, so stick with the start of the day.

Every day? You will have days when you don't get to your Start The Day List until midday, or even the end of the day. The key is once you catch your breath after responding to the urgent items that kept you from doing the list, take stock of your world and do the list. EXECUTE

> *"How you start often determines how you finish"*
>
> *- Anon*

EXECUTE Bonus: End of the Day – To create closure at the end of the day it helps to review the same checklist you used to Kickstart your day. It's nice to hear yourself say the word "finished!" for a sense of closure.

Pre-call Plan.

"You don't know if you are going to win or lose until you win or lose. So don't worry about it, focus on the preparation"

– John Calipari

Sales is no different. You don't know whether you will win or lose until you have won or lost. Until you have the order, the only thing which brings value is continuing to focus on the preparation of each interaction and then EXECUTE each item.

WHAT – While your final format may be different depending on your product or service, we have found there are three critical elements in every Pre-Call Plan:

- ☐ Objectives
- ☐ Questions
- ☐ Next Step

You can download our complimentary copy at www.salesoctane.com/resources/EXECUTE

HOW – Go back and identify every key interaction you have with prospects and customers. This may include trade shows, initial prospecting efforts, drop-ins, incoming inquiries, initial conversations (whether face to face, phone to phone, or screen to screen), presentations, demonstrations, proposal presentations/closes, account reviews, and the list goes on.

execute

These are just a few of the ones we have seen through the years. Once you have this list of engagements then create a typical Pre-call Plan for each of those scenarios.

Step 1: Objectives

Think of what success would look like. Ask the question "This sales call will be successful if I _____," and then whatever you put in the blank becomes a possible objective. Obviously closing the sale is an objective, however, this may be too early in the process.

You can reverse engineer each typical engagement to identify some objectives. Ask yourself the question: if this sales call goes sideways (you lose/fail to get what you want), why did you lose? What did you fail to do? Take that list and create your objectives so the problem is less likely to happen!

Check with others who have been selling your product or service and ask them the questions above. Seeking the wisdom of others is a key characteristic of the SalesPRO.

Most of our clients have the following objectives as they pursue any sales opportunity. Budget/Money, Identifying the Decision-maker, Identifying the Decision-making process, Timing, Building Rapport, Identifying needs and challenges and Confirming their current situation. The list is endless and depends entirely on your specific product, service and sales process. One thing is for sure. When you have Objectives, you are more likely to be prepared!

Step 2: Questions

One of your goals should be to get your customer talking. You learn very little when *you* are talking and, conversely, you can learn a lot when your customer talks. A great way to accomplish this is to have your questions ready in advance of the sales call. Simply take every objective you created in step 1 and develop at least one question or technique to accomplish this objective. While this may seem like a lot of work the reality is the questions will not change much over time because the objectives seldom change. So, once you or your team create the list of questions, it becomes much easier to create a Pre-call plan in very little time for subsequent sales calls.

Make sure your questions cannot be answered with a yes or a no. This keeps the customer sharing information and allows time for you to think as well as write notes. The key words to make your questions open-ended or assumptive are included on the form.

Finally, as you begin to EXECUTE the questions on future sales calls, take note of which ones work better than others. You may find that some of your questions just don't seem to be effective. Note this, and then figure out before your next call how to improve that question or technique. Finally, when you hear your customer occasionally say, "That's a good question," or "I've not thought about that," then you know your questions are working.

One thing leads to another – you can't summarize the results of an appointment in writing for a client if you don't take notes. You can't take notes if you are doing all the talking. You can't stop talking if the customer is answering with staccato yes and no answers. You won't ask open-ended questions if you did not prepare your questions in advance. Your best questions are the result of having targeted objectives for the sales call. This why the SalesPRO has a process to develop a brief pre-call plan with targeted objectives and high-gain questions. However, you have to cross the finish line with a clearly defined next step, which in order to move the sale forward.

execute

Step 3: Next Step

The end of every sales conversation arrives abruptly. Whether the sales call has gone good or bad, it is always the same. The customer looks at their watch, appears distracted by their mobile device, or mentions they have another meeting to get to and thank you for your time. You are stuck. You simply say thanks and confirm you will follow up later. The problem is Parkinson's Law.

Initially shared in a 1955 article in *The Economist*, Cyril Northcote Parkinson shared his theory, now referred to as Parkinson's Law: "Work expands to fill the time available for it's completion." Think about how you work the days and hours leading up to your vacation. You become focused and exceptionally efficient since you must complete the work before time runs out and you jump on the plane. This also explains why salespeople tend to get caught unaware at the end of a sales call when the customer is DONE, meaning time has run out, and there is no time to close for the next step. The SalesPRO understands this law and is always ready with their next-step approach whenever it arrives during the sales call.

WHAT – While what you say depends on where you are in your sales process we have typically found there are several typical scenarios:

- The first conversation where the next step would be a subsequent appointment.
- The subsequent appointment where the next step would be a demonstration or visit.
- The Demonstration/Visit where the next step would be a proposal.

- ☐ A proposal where the next step would be the close. (IF you did not close and changes were requested)
- ☐ The Follow up appointment where the revised proposal would be closed.
- ☐ The after-sale appointment where you would ask for referrals/reviews.

If your product or service has a long sales cycle with numerous meetings then you would have one step in this process which would just repeat each time.

HOW – Write it out. Yes, write it out word-for-word. The process of writing forces you to organize your thoughts. Once you write them out and say them aloud, you often realize they don't flow. So, continue to craft the language until the next-step statement is smooth and clear. In the process of organizing, writing and practicing the language, you begin to embed it into your brain.

WHEN – Once you have the language ready, and as soon as you sense the appointment is coming to an end, go directly to the next-step request. Watch how you comfortably move the sales process forward more often than in the past. The SalesPRO never goes into any selling situation without a clear idea of exactly how they will move the sale forward at the end of the conversation. This is why they have become the SalesPRO.

Checklist

You will notice the Checklist along the side of the Pre-call Plan. We will cover the checklist in Chapter 10 when we discuss flow and productivity. For now, just know that the SalesPRO has a checklist for everything they do on a repetitive basis.

execute

WHEN - When do you do a Pre-call Plan? Whenever you are planning to engage with a customer. As the saying goes, "those who fail to plan, plan to fail".

Account Strategy

Having an account strategy before you begin the sales process is now more essential than ever. Given the barriers your prospects have erected to limit access makes it essential to have a strategy before you engage. As we shared in *Selling by the Book Today*, prospects do homework before they engage with you, so once they agree to a conversation or even to taking your call, you must be far more relevant and impactful during the initial conversation. Bottom line, the SalesPRO does their due diligence before they begin their prospecting efforts because they understand their first connection may be their only chance! Plus, once you have a solid account strategy, the Pre-call plans for each engagement will fall into place and your confidence soars.

WHAT – AccountMap™. The type of information you require for an account strategy will depend on your product and service. Over the years, we gathered all the basic due diligence we saw our clients pursuing as we helped them create an account strategy. We then consolidated these basics into one document and we called it the AccountMap™. This prompts the SalesPRO for strategy information and allows you to organize your thoughts as you gather the due diligence. Then the AccountMap™ allows you to share your strategy with others and gain the insight, wisdom, knowledge and experience of your team in a far more focused manner.

You can view details of the AccountMap™ at www.salesoctane.com/resources/EXECUTE.

HOW - Identify all the information a salesperson would want to know about an account to have the best opportunity to win at each phase of your sales process. Begin with the AccountMap™ questions and add your unique needs based on your specific product or service. Have the salesperson fill out the information to the point where they have exhausted their knowledge.

Next, at a minimum, gather the sales team. It helps to include other stakeholders such as leadership and even other cross-functional roles within your company. Having non-selling roles participate accomplishes two things. First, others will often see and ask things the salesperson has not thought about. Second, it gives others in your organization an appreciation for the effort required to sell your solutions.

Once you have the group together, have the salesperson share their account strategy and solicit ideas from the team. In a very disciplined and written manner, capture the insight, knowledge and experience of the others. At the end of the process, the salesperson will have a number of new ideas they had not thought of prior to the brainstorming using the AccountMap™.

NOTE: Avoid making this the Spanish Inquisition. The easiest way to accomplish this is to reinforce that everyone on the team will present their AccountMap™ for one of their accounts over the course of the year. This sends the message to treat the others professionally in the process.

WHEN – The sooner you create an AccountMap™, the sooner you can organize your Account Strategy. The sooner you create your Account Strategy, the sooner you can share it with others. The sooner you share with others, the sooner you hear of new and innovative strategies to create a more robust sales strategy. And the sooner you have a robust sales strategy ,the sooner you are prepared to engage in the process as a SalesPRO.

"Make the month, make the quarter, make the year"

– Gary VanDyke

When I first began selling, I had a Sales Manager who repeated the mantra above. The bottom line is, if you make your month, you have a better chance of making the quarter... and if you make the quarter, you have a better chance of hitting your number for the year. In the case of the SalesPRO, they begin with making each day count. Each day leads to each sales call. Each sales call leads to each account strategy. So, work PROactively from both ends and you dramatically improve your odds of success!

Jim Ryerson

Think It, Ink It!!

■ **WHAT**

■ **HOW**

■ **WHEN**

Submit your best practices at the link below for the chance to have it featured as a Shot of Octane Video.
https://salesoctane.com/resources/best-practices/

The
Found in

PRO is PRiOrity

Chapter 9: The PRO is Found in PRiOrity

Chapter 9

The PRO is Found in PRiOrity

Activity matters!

If you are going to make the month, quarter and year, you will need to focus on your level of sales activity. Once again, if you follow the typical salesperson around for a day there is a lot of activity. It is like chasing a swarm of bees. Lots of buzz, erratic movement darting left and right and every so often, someone gets stung. *Activity* is a word which defines salespeople; however, the SalesPRO adds one more word to define their activity: *Targeted*.

Why? Targeted activity and planning takes time. The pre-call research, plans and account strategy all take time. In most cases, you picked up this book because you were looking for a way to deal with all the chaos and find some extra time. Now we just piled on PROactive planning, which takes time. The question is, where do you go to find hours to re-allocate to the planning and strategy thinking? The answer is found in reducing the amount of time spent chasing low probability situations. We won't even call them "opportunities" or "sales" because they are not opportunities and they rarely represent a sale. Even when you do occasionally win a sale with a less-than-ideal customer, they seem to take far more time than your best clients.

"When you say yes to something, you say no to something else"

– Michael Bramson.

In order to leverage your available hours, you will need to say yes to higher probability sales opportunities and no to anything that does not fit your ideal customer criteria. Later in this chapter, we provide some options on what to do when you recognize you are faced with, and are about to spend time on, an unqualified situation. For now, develop your ideal customer criteria so you can move toward saying yes to ideal prospects and no to the rest.

Begin by going back to your Pre-call plans from Chapter 8. What are the objectives you set for your sales calls or conversations? Regardless of the different variations: Cold call, Warm call, First Appointment, Demonstration, Closing, etc., go back and take a look at the objectives. What are the types of information you are looking for which would be a good indication that it is a qualified opportunity? Here are some qualification examples:

- ☐ You are able to confirm the name of the Decision-maker.
- ☐ You are able to communicate directly with the Decision-maker (no intermediary or gatekeeper).
- ☐ You are able to secure how they will make the decision and their steps align with your DecisionMap™.
- ☐ You are able to identify all the stakeholders who will be involved with your product or service.

execute

- You are given the budget.
- The budget fits with your solution.
- You confirmed their timing to move forward (they are not just out kicking the tires...they intend to buy).
- You identified a problem you can solve and the prospect confirmed the value of solving this problem.
- You established rapport.
- You confirmed they know and spoke with someone who has used your product or service in the past (referral).
- They are familiar with your company.
- They have used your company in the past and it was a good experience.
- Your values and their values align (personally and/or corporately)
- There is open communication between you and their team.
- You and your team will be able to present directly to the final decision maker.

Then, one last step, go back to your best practices from your AccountMap™ sessions and add additional criteria which could be used for evaluating prospects. Here are some additional qualification examples from AccountMap™ sessions we have done:

- The prospect is open to new ideas and insight.
- Your strengths align with their needs.
- Your weaknesses will not be an issue.

Jim Ryerson

- ☐ There is larger and long-term opportunity with the target.
- ☐ The target is a high-profile name in your space.
- ☐ There are no real threats known.
- ☐ The target is connected and willing to be a reference.
- ☐ The prospects behavior style is a good to excellent fit with your style.

These are just a few examples. There are many more which would be unique to your product or service. It is key you create a list of criteria so you can make wise choices of where to spend your time.

The PROfitable PROspect PROfile.

Often referred to as "scoring leads," the SalesPRO takes this criteria and uses it to evaluate or "score" potential targets, inquiries or leads before they expend too much of their precious time.

Oftentimes, salespeople do *not* take a few minutes to score their targets, and instead race forward, having fallen victim to something psychologists refer to as "cognitive closure." Cognitive closure is our desire for closure in the midst of confusion and uncertainty. So we just randomly fill in the blanks, often with irrational justification, and race off towards another low-probability situation. You've heard the statements around the office, "This could be huge!", or, "This could make my year!", or even, "This just came out of nowhere!" Oftentimes you will find the propensity for cognitive closure increases in frequency when a salesperson is brand-new, behind their goal, or really needs the commission. The SalesPRO manages their need for cognitive closure by scoring their targets and saying yes to PROfitable PROspects.

Driven by Fear, Optimism or a need for instant gratification?

In some cases your fear of being disliked makes it difficult to say no to an unqualified situation. You just don't want to disappoint someone who is looking for a solution to his/her problem. You may be an optimist and think you can make it work with your schedule. Or, you may just want to say yes so you get the instant gratification. The problem with instant gratification is it seldom lasts past that first instant. All three motivations are a trap. Just say no. When you say no to those situations that are not the best use of your time or energy, you will be saying yes to the high-probability targets who will fuel your referral stream in the future. Your time is limited, so limit it to working on qualified, high-probability and high pay-off opportunities.

PROceed? How to say no...

"When you say no to something, you say yes to something else"

– Jim Ryerson

How does a salesperson say no and still maintain a positive relationship? Remember, the prospects situation may change in the future causing them to become a qualified target. Or, the person you are speaking with may take a role at another company that is a qualified target. You want to maintain a relationship even when you say no. There are three basic options and a host of iterations.

Here are the main options:

1. Suggest another provider

The easiest option is to suggest this is not the best fit for you or your company and recommend they contact another provider. It's best if you can personally make the recommendation and tell them to use your name when calling the other provider. This leaves the client with a positive impression of you and allows them to get their problem resolved. Make sure you plug their information into your CRM and stay connected as things change down the line.

Occasionally, one of our clients will suggest these other providers may, to a minor extent, be a small competitor. What we often figure out after debating the option to send business to a competitor is if you keep your small competitor busy with small opportunities they rarely become a major competitor. The busier they are chasing around smaller targets then the less time they have for your ideal targets. When you say NO to unqualified targets you are saying YES to the larger qualified targets and you have the time and energy to service those accounts!

2. Leverage the power of scarcity – an incoming inquiry

Let's put this in perspective. You get a call and someone wants you to come out and take a look at his/her situation. On the surface it looks like a lead. You ask your qualification questions and it becomes clear with each answer this is not something you should spend your valuable time on.

Response: "I really can't take on another project at this time."

This statement sends the message you are in demand and have a lot going on. Here's the best part, they can't argue with this, as you are controlling the situation. Tell them this may change down the line, as it very possibly could! Then immediately either recommend another provider or perhaps move it to another person on your team. This could be a junior salesperson or inside sales. Make sure you plug their information into the CRM so someone at your company stays connected as things change down the line.

3. PROpose

Occasionally you may have an unqualified target who is both demanding and wants you to drop everything, or they are fine with waiting until you can get to them. In both cases, it is a trap. The best option is to make a profitable proposal on the spot and, if possible, ask for upfront payment to get the process started.

When we say, "propose on the spot (or on the call)," we literally mean give a highly profitable price or range right up front. This number must compensate you for your time and then some, because you know these unqualified leads are often fraught with unforeseen challenges. Ask for compensation for a portion of the project right then and there. It's policy. Be prepared to offer another provider's phone number as an option. Make sure you plug their information into the CRM as these types of targets tend to call back hoping to get someone else on the phone who is new to your company, behind quota or needs the commission.

Always leave these conversations with a reference to "things change," you're "always coming up with new options/insight," and "let's keep in touch." Because you have their information in CRM your down-stream marketing will keep them connected.

The absolute best solution to avoiding unqualified targets is to be actively engaged with qualified opportunities. The sting of saying "no" is quickly replaced with the energy and enthusiasm to focus your time, talents and resources on situations where you can make a difference and see your business grow at an exponential pace.

When you focus on qualified opportunities you position yourself for PROductivity and flow which will accelerate your sales!

execute
Think It, Ink It!!

■ WHAT

■ HOW

■ WHEN

Submit your best practices at the link below for the chance to have it featured as a Shot of Octane Video.
https://salesoctane.com/resources/best-practices/

PROductivity

=

+ Flow
SalesPRO

Chapter 10: PROductivity + Flow = SalesPRO

Chapter 10

PROductivity + Flow = SalesPRO

It's Moving Day!

In a professional golf tournament, the match runs from Thursday through Sunday, 18 holes a day, for 4 days. Saturday, the third day of the tournament, is often referred to as "moving day," as most players who have the opportunity to either enlarge their lead or pull themselves back into contention will attempt to make a move on Saturday.

Chapter 10 is moving day for the SalesPRO. If you are already having success, then this is where you enlarge your lead. If you are out of contention, then this is the chapter to move you back into the game as the SalesPRO.

The concepts in this chapter are simple. Notice I did not say *easy*. The definition of the word simple is "readily understood" while the definition of easy is "requiring little effort." You will have no challenge understanding the concepts in this section, as they are readily apparent to even the novice salesperson. The challenge is, these techniques and actions require a lot of effort and discipline. However, these simple concepts can move your results from ordinary to extraordinary as long as you EXECUTE.

What stops you from getting things done? What keeps you from entering a state of high focus and productivity, what we refer to as "flow?" You've consolidated your world of chaos to ONE PLACE as a result of implementing the ideas from Chapter 5. You have committed yourself to embracing your CRM after Chapter 6.

With the concepts from Chapter 7, you are managing your commitments and avoiding over-commitments because you have a better understanding of how your behavior style often got you into trouble in the past. You are developing a plan for each day, sales engagement and target account from Chapter 8. And after Chapter 9, you are equipped with great questions and a process to help you discern when to say yes, and how to say no.

There are a number of obstacles the SalesPRO must overcome in pursuit of productivity and flow. Let's start with diagnosing some of the pitfalls that can erode flow and productivity.

☐ Blind Optimism

Back in Chapter 2, we shared research that concludes that the Salespeople we have assessed since 2010 tend to be more extroverted and people-oriented (rather than task/detail-oriented and introverted), compared to the rest of the population.

The extroverted/people-oriented tendency often brings with it a blind optimism of how much they can accomplish in a given time. Is this you? How often do you finish the day wondering where the time went? Optimism is a wonderful characteristic as long as it does not blind you to reality.

Second, the lack of detail-orientation often results in under-estimating the amount of time or effort is required to complete a task. Combine the blind optimism of how much you can do with under-estimating the actual time required and you can see how quickly someone can fall out of flow and into a chaotic state of activity... which, as we have seen, is counterproductive.

execute

☐ Confusing multi-tasking for flow

Many salespeople claim that their ability to multi-task is a sign of strength. The SalesPRO, however, knows it is much more productive to focus and perform by concentrating on the task at hand with a clear mind. Multi-tasking is not what you think it is. The brain does not allow you to do two things at once without sacrificing flow[8].

Think of the last time you were driving down the highway to a familiar destination. You knew exactly which exit to take. At the same time, you took a phone call, and while concentrating on the conversation, you drove right past the exit. What happened? Conversely, think of the number of times you did not know where you were going. While you were attempting to look at the navigation display and even listen to the APP directions, you needed to interrupt a phone conversation with, "Hang on a second, I have to figure out which exit to take!" What is happening? Your brain can only concentrate well on one task at a time.

The term is called "flow"[9] and the SalesPRO lives in flow. You may in fact move rapidly between tasks but it is a fluid transition with one item being completed and then moving to the next versus the rapid fire back and forth.

Multi-tasking is a myth. Two tasks are not getting done at the same time with any level of proficiency. Multi-tasking, or busy-ness, is simply moving quickly from one task to the other, exchanging focus and performance for the illusion of "doing" business.

Busy is the enemy of EXECUTE.

---

[8] https://en.wikipedia.org/wiki/Human_multitasking
[9] Mihaly Csikszentmihályi (1990). *Flow: The Psychology of Optimal Experience*. Harper & Row. ISBN 978-0-06-016253-5

☐ Leaning into the punch

Salespeople are often the center of activity because of their pivotal role in driving revenue. The challenge becomes finding the space to complete those tasks which require solitude and thinking. Account Strategy, Call Plans and Projects of any kind require space to think. Being too available because of your pivotal role will diminish your effectiveness in the long run. This can become even more of a challenge if your brain is wired to crave the interruptions and activity. Do you crave the interaction and office chatter? If you are an extrovert you get energy from people which may explain some of the craving. While you may have good intentions, this can quickly become an obstacle to productivity.

Remember: You make time for what you make time for.

☐ Disdain for Rules

Do you love to follow rules made by others? The behavioral term is called "compliance" and our research indicates this is a behavior seldom embraced by the typical salesperson. For some reason, salespeople are not wired like an engineer or safety officer (unless, perhaps, you are a Sales Engineer). Here's the catch: rules are typically put in place for our own good. Following some simple rules in sales can have a profound impact on your productivity. The SalesPRO understands they can adapt their behavior in certain situations. They set aside their natural tendencies and trust the PROcess. When was the last time you did a pirouette back to your desk multiple times to grab something for an appointment? This may be a sign of not having

execute

a process in place or as is often the case not following the process. You may need to follow the rules.

☐ Absence of Sales Activity goals

We occasionally hear a Sales Manager or Leader say "I don't care what they do all day as long as they hit their sales goals!" The challenge with this logic is it takes time to see if you hit your sales goal. Depending on the sales cycle of your product or service, you may not really know until its months, quarters or even farther down the path. The SalesPRO achieves their Sales Goal because they set and focus on achieving the incremental Activity Goals that have proven over time (the rule) to yield results.

Every sale is a work in progress until the order is placed or the check is cleared. Oddly enough, the term "work in progress" is often referred to as W.I.P., which is really what activity goals become. They whip us into the actions that we know will yield sales results. How do you measure your progress? Incremental activity goals, or the all or nothing world of your sales goal?

☐ Big goals | Procrastination

In some cases we find salespeople with a sales goal or a goal for a project they need to complete and they are paralyzed where or how to start. So, they clean their office. Procrastination ensues and the sales goal or project goal continues to hover like a dark cloud of chaos.

☐ Waiting to Wait

When we are not in control of every sales encounter, we inevitably finish with an agreement to reconnect in a few days, weeks or months in order to set up the next appointment. The challenge is, we then spend needless time trying to get in touch with the other party to coordinate calendars and set the appointment.

Failing to confirm the next appointment at the end of a call will extend the sales process because of the time spent trying to connect in order to schedule the next step.

- **Not controlling your "work" schedule (because you don't know it)**

Think of the last time you said, "Let me get back to you once I check my schedule." Back to the inefficiency of attempting to schedule the next step. What is the barrier to always having your schedule in front of you and up to date?

- **Unable to take full advantage of your availability**

Downtime. Usually, the only time we have downtime to think is when someone is late for an appointment. You arrive early and then wait 20 minutes past the scheduled time before they arrive. Oddly enough, unless you are organized, you cannot take advantage of these opportunities. Because of the chaos we discussed at the start of this book, these late arrivals will become more frequent. How are you organized and positioned to take advantage of these multiple blocks of downtime which occurs every day?

The How & What of flow and productivity!

execute

Now that we know some of the barriers to PROductivity and flow we want to turn our attention to what we need to modify and how to get started.

☐ **Remove Physical distractions**

Take control of your physical environment to gain flow. Begin with doing everything you can to reduce the clutter that is often a visual distraction. There are plenty of great books on organization and they all begin with putting everything in one pile and then creating some sort of filing system to put things away until you need them. Out of sight helps keep clutter out of your mind.

Continue with your computer desktop since this is just the new version of the physical desktop. Your main screen should be clear of files and folders and images. The only reason they are there is because you have not put them in an organized system. If you continue to let the desktop icons accumulate then you become far less efficient as you have another place for content to accumulate.

If you have the opportunity to close a door, close it. Put a door hanger which says DO NOT DISTURB when you have to focus on a project. As long as you are hitting your sales goal, no one is going to complain. Talk about this with your support team so everyone begins to focus. If you have an Extroverted/People-oriented behavior style this can be an out-of-body experience. You will begin to notice that when you stay away from the office chatter, you minimize the proverbial monkey being placed on your back.

"Not my circus, not my monkey"

- Polish proverb

This may begin to sound monastic; however, it works. Even noise is a distraction for many of us. If you have the opportunity to wear noise-canceling headphones while you focus on your task, then take advantage of the white noise. For instance, this entire book was written next to the ocean. Well, not exactly. The neuropsychologist I've been working with the past 2 years suggested it best to listen to something I was not familiar with, so that the noise was just white noise. Humming to your favorite music is a form of multi-tasking in the brain. Opt for something that is simply white noise so you can concentrate. I opted for the sound of ocean waves.

☐ **Remove remaining distractions including notifications.**

You know what this means, and you will resist until you spend 30 minutes without distraction and experience the difference. Take a project that you estimate will take 30 minutes. Before you begin to EXECUTE, get into a physical situation free of distraction. Then—and here comes the fun part—turn off every notification on every digital device you have. This means phone notifications, computer desktop notifications, alarms, reminders, etc. You will begin to go through withdrawal as you begin your project. Just focus on the project and you will enter flow.

"Think about what you think about"

- Anon

As soon as you have a notification go off and you look at it you are out of flow and the residual thoughts with the notification will take several minutes to forget—if you can even forget. If you

execute

jump on the notification you will jump out of flow and chaos ensues.

NOTE: you will think of things during this "notification free" time. When you think it, ink it...but don't take it any farther. It will be there when you finish your project!

☐ Be Realistic

It is entirely possible that during the 30-minute exercise we just mentioned, you will realize the task takes a lot longer than 30 minutes to complete. It's your optimism, and optimism is a strength. The best way to reduce the over commitments, disappointment and chaos which accompany blind optimism is to keep track of how long it took.

In chapter 8 we introduced the concept of the Focus 5. Step 5 in the process is to review the disparity between how long you projected something would take and how long it actually took. You will find as much as a 30% disparity, and it's never in the direction you want. We massively underestimate how long it will take to complete routine tasks. Once we set daily task goals, assign our projected timing and then review the actual result we begin to manager our optimism and make more realistic commitments.

☐ One Place

In chapter 5 we shared the concept of limiting the number of places information can accumulate. This dramatically reduces wasted time spent looking for things once you have limited your available options. Email folders, Digital notes and a consistent organized computer are critical because looking for displaced items is a massive blow to flow.

☐ Signatures/Templates

Think about the number of times you send the same email content or message to someone. You retype the same thing over and over again. In many cases you go back to your SENT folder and find a similar message you sent to someone else, copy the content and then modify it slightly for the new recipient before you send it off. Think about the wasted time, brainpower and frustration since often when you go into the sent folder you will see something else which reminds you of another problem you need to resolve. This is an easy fix. The answer is to use either a built-in template for your mail or messaging application or simply create separate signatures with the routine email content you send.

You can see an example at
www.salesoctane.com/resources/EXECUTE

☐ Recurring entries

Stop spending your valuable brainpower trying to remember. Instead, put recurring reminders in your CRM so you don't have to remember! This can range anywhere from a reminder to check in with a key client quarterly all the way to remembering to send in your weekly expense report. Once you have all the recurring tasks and reminders in your CRM calendar, you will be less inclined to pursue unqualified targets and make over-commitments because you are reminded of what you have to do because you see it daily!

Our brains play tricks on us. We think we've spoken with a target account about a month ago, however, it's actually been two months. When the recurring reminder pops up 30 days from now you will often exclaim, "Wow, has it already been a month?" This is a teachable moment. Yes, it has been a month and now you are going to do what you say you will do and give them a call. Your competitor will wait another 3-4 weeks.

☐ Checklists

In Chapter 8, PROactive, we referenced the Checklist on the Pre-call plan. Checklists are the disdain of most salespeople because they believe a checklist is beneath them. Humility is a key characteristic of the SalesPRO and as a result they humble themselves and embrace the checklist. Think of the times you head out the door only to pirouette and head back in because you forgot something. This is a major waste of time.

Instead, create a checklist for everything you routinely do. This is why pilots diligently run through their checklist regardless of how many flights they have flown. From the rookie on their first flight to the seasoned captain on their last flight before retirement, they all complete the same checklist. It gives them the internal locus of control and allows them to focus on the task at hand. I personally have 16 checklists with everything from packing for a trip to launching a screen share to the 60 minutes before I go on-stage to speak. Don't waste your valuable time trying to remember what to bring or what to do. If you do it frequently then there should be a checklist.

☐ Leverage screen-share technology

This may cause some consternation for our legacy salespeople. First, the issue is balancing time and opportunity. Clearly, it is best to be face-to-face with a customer. However, with increasing committee decisions and multiple stakeholders on the customer side, we often face the issue of gathering the entire group in order to engage with the customer. Add to this the reality of being in different cities, countries and time zones, and you both complicate and slow down the sales process. Screen-share sales calls are becoming an efficient way for the salesperson to engage their customers, regardless of the number and location, in a visual manner and speed up the sale.

It's a win-win. The customer does not have to drive or coordinate numerous geographic challenges, and you save on resources and time. You get to the customer sooner and with the video capability you can still see their body language as you go through the conversation. Screen-sharing including video is not for the faint of heart. It requires a clean computer desktop (see above), a checklist to make sure you are ready to go, and, as with all things, plenty of practice.

☐ Leading vs. Lagging indicators

Every salesperson has a sales goal. It may be a profitability goal or some other measurement which the company uses to define their ultimate success for the year. We call this a lagging indicator because it lags behind the actual process to secure the sale. The SalesPRO goes one step farther and breaks their annual sales goal down into the granular activities and tasks to secure the sale. These are called leading indicators. Examples may include qualified leads, appointments, presentations, proposals, etc. When I wrote *The First 100 Days of Selling* and *The First 100 Days of In-home Selling*, we put the metrics together around these critical activities. Once you have the leading indicators defined, they go directly into your CRM PROcess as automated reminders, tasks and next steps. Now you are prepared to EXECUTE and

execute

know with confidence your efforts and activity are targeted toward success.

"What gets measured gets done"

- Anon

☐ Break it down

Similar to breaking down a sales goal to the specific activities and tasks required to achieve the goal the same applies to any project you undertake. A few minutes of planning will help you EXECUTE at a faster pace. Break it down to those activities that need to happen in order to complete the project. Here are a few questions to ask before you race off:

- 🙂 What do I need to do first?
- 🙂 What do I need to do next/after that? (And then continue with question 2 over and over again until you have planned out the project)
- 🙂 Do I have what I need to complete the first task on the list? If not, back to question 1.

This takes time and effort, which is why cleaning the office suddenly becomes quite appealing. Don't fall victim to the illusion of activity=results. Targeted activity=results! Remember: diagnose the problem, plan the best route and EXECUTE.

☐ CLICKING away

Now that you have your leading indicators and tasks built into your CRM, you will spend less time trying to figure out what to do next and more time focused and in flow around key sales tasks. We call it CLICKING because a lot of the noise you will hear is the click of your mouse as you complete a task. These CLICKS reinforce your progress in much the same way crossing off a task on your day planner used to do. And, because it is in your CRM, you can measure it and modify your leading indicators based on actual results. Get clicking!

☐ Chunk your time

As you work toward being more focused you will notice there are certain times of the day and days of the week when you are better at certain tasks. These work cycles are unique to you personally and you need to figure out the best days of the week and times of the day to complete your key tasks. The goal would be to determine the best time for your key leading indicator activities.

In some cases your customers have better days and times to connect or meet, which also needs to be taken into consideration. The discretionary time will begin to get smaller in your work calendar. Toss in your personal realities with when you can start your day and when you have to be home, and you have even less discretionary time. The SalesPRO begins with their personal reality (family first) and then chunks out the best time to engage with their customers so they can EXECUTE their key leading indicators involving customers. Finally they fill in the remaining time with their tasks and they build them around their most productive work cycle if at all possible. When you're done with this you will have very little discretionary time available in your calendar. This reduces over-commitment and reinforces the importance of pursuing qualified opportunities.

EXECUTE Bonus: Shorten your meetings by selecting 15 minutes vs. a "half hour", 30 minutes vs. an "hour" or 90 minutes vs. a "couple hours." Use Parkinson's Law to your advantage!

☐ **Always carry a Pre-call Plan**

To reduce over-commitments, make sure to have your pre-call plan from Chapter 8 with you at all times. It can be a digital or physical copy, but you must have the objectives, questions and next steps always available. This way you know what questions to ask in order to achieve your objectives, qualify the opportunity and determine how to proceed to your next step.

Over the next few weeks and months you will begin to realize how much wasted time you spent going back to ask questions you should have confirmed when you were talking with the customer. All of these questions in your pre-call plans for each stage in your sales cycle will help you become very proficient when you get an unplanned call.

☐ **Always have a next step**

By having your pre-call plans with you then you already have a defined approach to asking for the next step. This will move the sale forward faster at each stage in the sales cycle. Make sure you have it with you and you will always leave every sales conversation with the next appointment confirmed.

☐ One calendar, always with you

In order to set the next appointment you must have your updated calendar with you at all times. This should be easy if you have gone with the One Place approach outlined in chapter 5. And, if it is aligned with your CRM, you are positioned to avoid committing to a time frame which was just booked by your Manager or team member in your CRM!

☐ Take advantage of every available minute

You are on time for your appointment and the other person is running behind. What do you do? The SalesPRO always takes advantage of downtown, even if it is simply to take a moment and breathe.

The SalesPRO has options and takes advantage of these short pockets of available time, instead of getting frustrated and anxious about how their day is about to implode. As the SalesPRO you can:

- ☐ Take a look at your Focus 5 and spend a few minutes getting some work done on a high priority task.
- ☐ Open up a digital book and gather additional learning in an area of expertise or skill you plan to hone.
- ☐ Write a digital thank you note to someone on your team or a customer.
- ☐ Run through your notes from the last few appointments or conversations and organize your thoughts while still

fresh in your mind (this is much easier to do with digital notes)
- [ ] Check your calendar for a call you can make while waiting.
- [ ] Hit the breathe app on your digital device and reduce stress and anxiety.

- [ ] **Dual purpose – two giants, one stone**

There is a difference between multi-tasking and multi-purposing your time. Given the fact the SalesPRO is always investing in new information and knowledge, here are some multi-purpose opportunities you can EXECUTE:

- [ ] Listen to digital learning content (books, podcasts, training, etc.) while you are working out.
- [ ] During your commute, listen to digital learning content or, if a passenger, pick something from the list above.
- [ ] Think. Take out your digital scratchpad and think through a project or idea by organizing your thoughts.
- [ ] Complete a pre-call plan for an upcoming sales call. The earlier you begin the plan, the more new ideas you will think of as it gets closer, and you can reduce your anxiety.
- [ ] Never eat alone. Simple approach to multi-purpose. Everyone has to eat. You, those who support you at your company and your customers. This takes planning; however, you have your calendar, so make the effort and ask someone to lunch!

- ☐ Walking meetings. This is a great way to think more creatively and get some much-needed movement. "Let's go for a walk and talk through this!"

☐ **Delegate/Outsource**

Depending on your situation, this approach is becoming more common even with salespeople who are working for a company. If you are self-employed, it is a great option to outsource some of those mundane tasks which you are neither proficient at nor love to do. There are numerous options, and you can get started by searching: Outsource Administrative Assistant.

"There is no try, only do!"

– Yoda, Star Wars

Start!

If you are going to exercise every morning, you improve the probability of taking the first step if you have your running shoes next to your bed. It's no different with every item in this chapter. The term "Incite action" means deciding what has to happen to get things moving with the new habit. Figure out what the trigger is and EXECUTE the first step. Momentum will build and the new routine will begin to take shape. Soon you will see the reward and a new habit begins to form.

"There is no try, only do… and then follow through!"

execute

– Jim Ryerson, Real Life

Finish!

As you begin to implement the ideas in this chapter, you may be tempted to give up and move to something else which is easier to complete. Stay with the task until you finish. Until you implement the routines and learn the new habits you literally cannot get to the finish line. Push through, keep moving forward, expend the extra effort and before long, your new routines become habit and those new habits will generate focus, productivity, flow, increased sales and raving customers who are willing to recommend you to others!

This is the reward for your effort!

Jim Ryerson

Think It, Ink It!!

■ **WHAT**

■ **HOW**

■ **WHEN**

Submit your best practices at the link below for the chance to have it featured as a Shot of Octane Video.
https://salesoctane.com/resources/best-practices/

PROspect & Go

PROmote Together

Chapter 11: PROspect & PROmote Go Together

Chapter 11

PROspect & PROmote Go Together

On the surface this makes sense. Prospecting is, to a certain extent, a form of promotion. However, the reason we put the two together goes far deeper than simply making more calls and being better at promoting your capabilities. This is about who is best to promote your capabilities and how you can accomplish your sales goals with fewer calls.

The process of getting in front of a prospect or simply having a conversation with a customer will continue to become increasingly more difficult. Phones go unanswered, your emails are relegated to spam and "No Soliciting" signs replace a receptionist or assistant you used to be able to charm. Phone-blocking technology now leads to unreturned prospecting voice mails and text even though you, the salesperson, never has a clue that you have been blocked. Customers all of a sudden leave for a new position at another company and you begin all over again.

The SalesPRO sees what is on the horizon and is hyper-focused on being "good" and connected. They leverage the transfer of trust. This will increase the probability of a conversation occurring sooner and move the sale faster than their unsuspecting competitors. So, what do you do?

☐ **Build your reputation**

Recently, a client of mine mentioned they had hired a Reputation Manager for their company. In all of my years of experience in the business world, I had never heard of this specific job title before, and I inquired, exactly, what a Reputation Manager does. Bottom line is, they scrape all forms of media for mention of the company and its leadership. Then, if it is a positive reference, they forward the information to someone else in their organization to leverage the good news.

However, when it is negative, they immediately go to work to halt the spread of the news, mitigate the damage and, if possible, convert the situation from a negative to a positive. In many cases the negative reference was inaccurate, and in some cases, dishonest—an effort to discredit the institution or even gain unrealistic compensation. This is the world we live in.

☐ **Be "good"**

The SalesPRO must be his/her own Reputation Manager. Using various free social media tools such as Google Alerts, Talkwalker Alerts and others, you can easily keep track of you and your company's reputation. As we shared in *Selling By the BOOK Today*, being seen as "good" or having a good reputation in your space is becoming more critical. Your prospects check you out on various sites once you begin the prospecting process whether you email, text, call or stop by. As soon as they hear your name they will look you up.

On the other hand, if the prospect is doing their own search on what solutions are available—before you are even aware of their interest—then it is possible their search will eventually lead all the way to you! This is why the SalesPRO is so focused on having a "good" reputation.

You can control your behavior, actions and even effort, but you have less control over their consequences. So, control the controllables!

execute

☐ Leverage your reputation

In all of our programs, we mention the importance of being "good" and connected. You have to be both! It is clearly a problem if a salesperson is connected and not "good." They are on a highway to a place where no salesperson wants to go.

However, it is even more tragic if a salesperson is "good," but not connected. They have put forth the effort to earn a good reputation, however, if they are not connected then they will not achieve the success they have earned.

So what do you do to become more connected and leverage your "good" reputation to accelerate your prospecting efforts?

☐ Build your brand image

The SalesPRO understands they have a brand. You have a brand. Think about if you had a company and it was called YOU, Inc. What would your social media page project to your prospects and customers? How easy would it be for someone to understand what you do, who you do it for, and what others think of you and your product or service? How easy have you made it for others to find and get in touch with you? This is a moving target, as social media sites change on a continuing basis. The SalesPRO routinely evaluates what new and improved concepts are being used to build their brand.

☐ Expand your network

The concept is called social expanding vs. social narrowing, and the SalesPRO is all about expanding their social network. From Associations, Non-profits and Social groups to Circles of

Influence, Vendors, Trade groups, Value-added Partners and everyplace between, the SalesPRO is actively expanding their network. Our first two books, *First 100 Days of Selling* and *First 100 Days of In-home Selling* go into greater detail with resources to improve your networking skills.

☐ Expand and share knowledge

As the PROfessor of Sales you have a lot of new knowledge. Once you begin helping others by sharing this knowledge, your reputation will expand. Using the power of familiarity others will begin to recognize your name and the value you bring because they see you engaged in their space on a consistent basis. You become familiar.

☐ Get connected

Once you link your CRM with social selling sites like LinkedIN® and others, you will accelerate your networking efforts. This demands you follow through by both putting their information in CRM and connecting with them on the social selling sites. The more connections you have, the easier it will be to find someone who knows and trusts you, and who is connected to your prospect. You are "good," you are "connected," and now you are about to be rewarded!

☐ Give - You first! PROmote others

When you meet someone else who sells, always be ready to give them new connections. Begin by understanding what they are selling and how you can help them get connected with other potential customers. The challenge is, when we ask others to

execute

explain what they sell, they pitch us on their product or service. The SalesPRO goes about this differently and asks questions to determine who *their* ideal customer is and what to look for and listen for which would be a good indication of a lead. And when the SalesPRO is asked what they do...they move quickly from what they do for others to who their typical client is and the challenges they face.

For anyone you meet, including someone who sells, we use the acronym L.I.N.K. to identify the four levels of information you need to identify in order to be able to help them.

> L = What **L**ine they are in
> I = Their **I**nterests
> N = Their **N**eeds, both personal and professional
> K = What and Who do they **K**now.

You can find more about L.I.N.K. in our books and on the Shot Of Octane app

☐ **Confirm the value**

Upon completion of every project, go back to your customer, confirm that you met (or exceeded!) their expectations, and then document the result. This is a crucial step in the sales process that many salespeople miss. They are working so hard on their next opportunity that they forget this very important task. The SalesPRO goes back and confirms with the customer that they have received value, and then they ask for referrals, reviews and recommendations.

☐ Ask

There are only two reasons you are not getting referrals: 1) you don't deserve them, or 2) you don't ask. Confirming value in the previous step addresses the first issue so you know you deserve the referral. In most cases it is simply the fact you are not asking.

Depending on your product or service, this may include reviews, recommendations and referrals. If you are asking for reviews on social media review sites or recommendations on networking sites, we have included some options at www.salesoctane.com/resources/EXECUTE. But beware, these sites often alter their processes.

Asking for referrals requires planning and technique. We provide several options on how to prepare and ask for referrals on our free Shot Of Octane app. Just search the word: REFER and watch the videos.

You may be asking for referrals within the company to build share of wallet, or asking for referrals outside of their company for new sales leads. Either way, you will see a referral prospect or "warm lead" move faster through the prospecting efforts to the first conversation and all the way to the close.

☐ PROspect – Who PROmotes is critical

execute

Having your satisfied customers share how you have helped them is far more impactful than you telling a prospect how you have helped others. The term is called "social proof." When your satisfied customer posts positive proof about your product, service and even you personally, then the claims are far more meaningful and trustworthy than if they come solely from you. Pointing your potential customers to what others are saying creates the transfer of trust from your customer to your prospect.

When your satisfied customer shares the name of a possible referral, ask if you can use their name in your prospecting efforts to warm up the otherwise cold call. The difference between a warm call and a cold call is exponential.

Cold Call	Warm Call
• Requires connecting at the right time.	• Already been pre-qualified for need.
• Requires many attempts before there is any hope the prospect will feel inclined to reward your persistence.	• Takes fewer attempts simply because the prospect does not want to disappoint their colleague who shared the name, especially if your customer called the prospect to let them know to expect a call from you.
• Has an element of distrust built into the equation	• Has an element of trust, the transfer of trust
• Pre-call research is limited to what you can find.	• Has the insight from the referrer as part of the pre-call research.

Ask for referrals and accelerate your prospecting and sales process! Once you close, you can begin the process all over

Jim Ryerson

again with documenting value, generating more social proof and securing more referrals. This is why the sales funnel is so old school. You need to think in terms of the Sales Continuum!

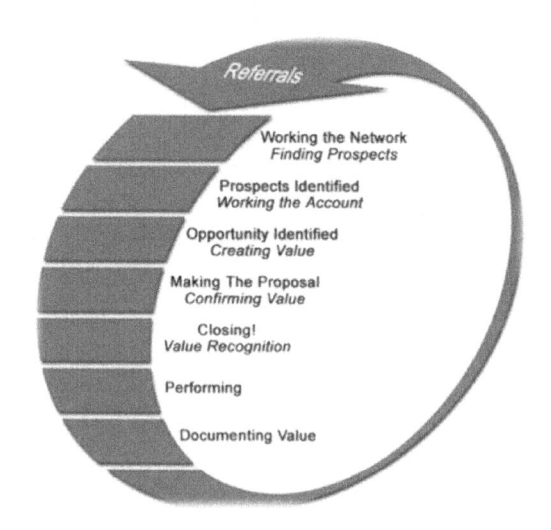

Referrals
- Working the Network / Finding Prospects
- Prospects Identified / Working the Account
- Opportunity Identified / Creating Value
- Making The Proposal / Confirming Value
- Closing! / Value Recognition
- Performing
- Documenting Value

Sales Continuum™

☐ PROcess

Each of the steps in this chapter are easy to forget in the chaos of daily sales activity. This is why the SalesPRO will incorporate the steps for each of these critical tasks into their PROcess. Go back through the chapter and identify where you can leverage recurring entries, checklists, planning tools and CRM so you don't spend valuable brainpower trying to remember what to do next—and instead you EXECUTE!

execute

Think It, Ink It!!

■ WHAT

■ HOW

■ WHEN

Submit your best practices at the link below for the chance to have it featured as a Shot of Octane Video.
https://salesoctane.com/resources/best-practices/

PROvide Brain

– Body, & Energy

Chapter 12: PROvide – Body, Brain & Energy

Chapter 12

PROvide —Body Brain & Energy

When you, the SalesPRO, drive the sales process, your body is the vehicle and your brain, the engine. When you take care and tune up your brain and body for peak performance, it is only natural you will EXECUTE at a higher level.

We'll start at the top. Your brain. As many self-help books reinforce, the average human being only uses about 10% of their brain capacity. So, everything we have covered to this point in the book should be relatively easy to learn and implement given the 90% latent brainpower available. This book would have really been easy had this been the case.

However, this 10% brain use statement, falsely attributed to Albert Einstein and others through the decades, is incorrect. It is an urban legend. The fact is, we use 100% of our brain throughout the day. So, now what? Enter my new favorite word— "plasticity." Plasticity is used to define the brains ability to change. Even though the brain stops "growing" in your mid-20s, research confirms that the brain is capable of significant change and improvement over your lifetime…with effort. Repeat—with effort.

While there are a myriad of opinions on what, specifically, you should do to improve your brain performance, we are only going to take the obvious. When creating this chapter, I decided to go from the easiest to the most difficult so you can get some early rewards, and this will keep moving you down the list.

☐ Hydrate

Just drink more water. There is a very high probability you are dehydrated as you read this sentence. Think about the typical daily drill of the salesperson. Wake up, consume coffee/tea to jump-start the day. Grab a bagel and additional coffee at the drive-thru window. Get to the office, consume more coffee. Middle of the day you need the jolt, so you reach for either a caffeinated beverage, an energy drink or more coffee. And for those of you who spurn the energy drink, please realize your typical brew from the Coffee Shop typically contains more caffeine than the energy drink.

Now go to the end of the day. That glass of wine, beer, cocktail—more dehydration. You don't need to be a Puritan; you just need to drink more water. If you expect your brain to participate in the typical day in the life of a salesperson, it will crave water ! Why? When you are dehydrated you don't think clearly[10] and the SalesPRO needs clarity in the brain.

Everyone has their theory on how much is enough, and you should check with your physician (add it to your list for your annual check-up as they will be very impressed with the question). However, lets just go with the common refrain on most of the WEB Physician sites which is…it depends. Sorry. It depends on weight, activity, where you live in terms of climate and a host of other variables, which is why you need to add it to the list for your Physician. Go to the web and search a reputable site and select the calculation you wish!

---

[10] Popkin B, D'Anci K, Rosenberg I. Water, hydration, and health. *Nutr Rev.* 2010;68(8):439-458

☐ **Move.**

Move sounds easier than *exercise*, which is why I use it to lure you in. Bottom line is, your brain responds very well to exercise especially if you are easily distracted... Squirrel! Plus, you will consume more water. You can see how these habits build on each other.

Backstory: I grew up wearing HUSKY clothing. It was code for *fat*, although I was led to believe it was a fashion tag. Unfortunately, I was not an athlete in school, which resulted in more bulk. In early 2015, while on deadline to complete *Selling by the BOOK Today*, I stumbled into some research on the positive impact of exercise on the ability to mentally focus. This was critical, as writer's-block had settled in, and it was chaos. This led to the acquisition of a Personal Trainer and I will never, willingly, go back to the bad old days.

Be honest, the greatest barrier to engaging in exercise is time. You are too busy with the demands of work and family, which consume all available time in your schedule. Here's the catch: when you exercise, you EXECUTE at a much higher level, which in turn creates time in your schedule to, yes, exercise. This is a self-fulfilling process. Keep exercising, keep EXECUTING at a high level. Reduce exercise, chaos occurs.

The challenge with exercise is its failure to provide results right away. You will be excited when you purchase the trendy exercise outfit, cool shoes, and digital monitors and download multiple exercise apps to your device. Adrenaline kicks in when you first walk towards your personal trainer, into the health club or simply walk onto the street and press the start button. Then reality sets in. It gets worse before it gets better. The SalesPRO makes the commitment, puts the plan in place, perseveres through the pain until the rewards begin to accrue and the habit sets in.

☐ Play & Rest

Your body and your brain need rest in order to perform when it matters. The SalesPro has downtime in order to restore his/her mind and body. This may include play, sports, hobbies, hanging out with friends, or just not doing anything! The key is to put it in your schedule or it will get pushed out by the incessant needs and distractions of the world.

Change your attitude about rest & play. Move from "I don't have time to play" to "I *must* take time to play." Remember the multi-purpose approach to walking meetings at the end of chapter 10? It also works when you take a break and take a walk. Many of the great thinkers say they have their best new ideas while taking a walk.

More and more of the sales conventions I am asked to speak at are building in downtime for the SalesPRO. It's amazing how often I hear positive stories of amazing connections, conversations and insight the SalesPRO gains during the downtime. This is no different in life. When we get off-task from our selling role, our brain opens up to explore and grow.

"Tell me what you eat and I will tell you what you are"[11]

- Anthelme Brillat-Savarin

---

[11] Physiologie du Gout, ou Meditations de Gastronomie Transcendante, 1826

☐ Nutrition

Fuel for your brain. On most days, the SalesPRO moves at the speed of sound. While the goal of this book is to slow down the pace while accelerating sales and profitability, the change will not happen overnight. So, in the meantime we continue to race between appointments and conversations and grab food whenever and wherever we can. I am literally the worst person to provide insight on nutrition so I will simply recommend you find a nutrition coach and EXECUTE a plan for improving what you eat.

☐ Sleep

Sleep gets a bad rap. It's not uncommon to hear someone brag about their ability to "only need 4-5 hours of sleep a night." Here's the reality: if you constantly short-change quality and quantity of sleep, it will have an adverse impact on your ability to think. Creativity, focus and a host of other positive characteristics suffer, and you cannot get it back over a weekend.

Distractions in the life of a salesperson are often at the core of a poor sleep regimen. Glued to our digital device right up until we turn off the light, we head off to bed with chaos scheming in our brain. Since your brain works while you sleep, why not use this time to have it "work" on the positive and not stew in the deadlines, disasters and challenges which will be there tomorrow. If you get a quality night's rest, you will be more far more capable in the morning.

Here is my personal Top 10 list to fuel your sleep!

10. Have a consistent bedtime
This is driven by our circadian rhythm[12]. Attempts to "power sleep" fail because they are off the rhythm. This is why traveling between time-zones is so challenging on quality sleep. Do your best to have a consistent bed-time and your body and brain will get into the rhythm.

9. Exercise
When you physically exert yourself with exercise during the _day_ (not prior to when you plan to head off to sleep) you will sleep better at night. Your body is tired which leads to better-quality sleep.

8. Hydrate
This all goes together, so when you exercise you consume more water. On average we lose between 1-1.5 pounds—yes, *pounds*—of water when we sleep. If you are dehydrated when you head off to bed, you have to get up during the night because you are parched and your sleep is interrupted. Or you wake up in the morning at less than 100%. If you are well-hydrated during the day, then you are set for a better night's sleep. Note: while obvious, trying to catch up on hydration right before you head off to bed will create its own challenge during your sleep cycle—so plan ahead to stay hydrated *during the day!*

7. Avoid caffeine
Avoid it like the plague 6 hours before you head off to bed. The residual of caffeine is there for many hours after you

---

[12] https://www.sleepfoundation.org/sleep-topics/what-circadian-rhythm

execute

consumed your elixir, interrupting quality sleep. Add the sponge-like effect it has on your hydration, and your brain becomes a desert.

6. Manage what, how much and when you eat
Much like alcohol, the monster meal or heavy foods close to bedtime gives the illusion of rest. Lying there with the food-baby may cause you to doze; however, the rest of the night is basically tossing and turning with little rest for your body or brain.

5. Avoid alcohol
Much like a big meal, alcohol will relax your brain and body. You feel tired which gives you the illusion the nightcap is literally a good night cap! The actual rest you get in this state is less than ideal. And, once the alcohol wears off, you wake up and it's hard to get back to quality rest. You're dehydrated and your brain is mush. Not good.

4. Cool down
When your sleeping space is too warm you sacrifice quality sleep. Go online to find which temperature range is best. I keep our space at 60 degrees Fahrenheit. It works.

3. Avoid the screen
Do not look at a computer screen, digital screen or television screen 90 minutes prior to heading off to bed. Go online and read the research on how LED screens mess with your rest—just not right before bedtime. Not an option? Then at least get a set of blue-light-blocking glasses.

2. Bedside note pad

Keep a note pad and a writing utensil next to your bed, so when you wrestle with a thought of something you need to remember to do, an idea to overcome a challenge, etc. Once you get it out of your brain and onto the note pad you can forget about it, because you know it will be there in the morning. Remember, your brain continues to work even when you are sleeping. Out of sight, out of mind is not true. The image is still there in your mind, messing with your rest. When you think it, ink it, so you can go back to sleep!

1. Meditative vs. Active Routine

Find your best approach for closing down your brain as you head off to sleep. Your brain continues to process during your sleep cycle so what you do before you turn out the lights makes a big difference. Head off to bed and sleep in the right frame of mind. Reading (not from your digital device), meditating or just closing your brain down from the day becomes a rhythm which triggers your brain to initiate sleep. Easing into rest becomes a routine and your brain learns the routine over time.

☐ **Your Brain**

Check out your most valuable asset

In May 2017, I decided to go to a Psychologist/Clinical Neuropsychologist to be assessed for attention challenges. After going through several tests over a series of appointments, the verdict was not a real surprise, especially to my wife, children and those who work with me: Attention Deficit / Hyperactivity Disorder. My question was direct: "What can I do to improve...

execute

without medication?" What you are reading in this chapter is a summary of the changes I have made to cope with distraction.

When you have any type of medical challenge, you throw yourself into research. Living on-line, continually searching for some insight or answer to improve your situation. Basically searching for hope. I was no different and read books on ADHD, focus and listened to everything I could find, including on-line videos and Ted Talks from experts on how to improve my situation. Then a fortuitous encounter dramatically improved my situation.

In May 2018, I had a conversation with someone I'd not seen for 30 years. We had lost track of each other due to a move out-of-state and our families being at different stages. He had reached out regarding training for some team members, so we met at one of their locations to chat. During the conversation, I divulged I had just been diagnosed with ADHD. He responded "You may *think* you have ADHD, but I'll bet you actually have *fast brain*." This was not a term I had heard before, so I took him up on his bet. I lost the bet and won back my brain.

☐ Get your brain in the range

With blood pressure you want to be in the range, the middle. Above the healthy range you end up with high blood pressure. Below the healthy range you end up with low blood pressure. Both high and low blood pressure have their own challenges and the treatments are different.

Your brain waves are no different. Without getting into too much detail, there is a healthy range where you want your brain waves to function. If they are too fast, they are above the range (think "not good" or "continuously chased by a bear"). If they are too slow, they are below the range (think "not good" or "easily distracted"). Whether you are above the healthy range (fast waves) or below the healthy range (slow waves), the clinical test for ADHD will provide the same outcome. Your symptoms will look the same. You have "ADHD." Options? Medication, do what's in this chapter, or both.

That's how I lost the bet and won my brain back. There is another option. Back to plasticity of the brain. The brain *can* change, and you *can* change it. If you have a clinician take a look at your brain waves, you can actually see whether they are above or below the range. The good news is, brain waves can be trained to move back into a healthy range. It takes a long time and it takes a fair amount of effort.

It may not work for everyone, however, it worked for me and it is working for countless others, including professional athletes. Think about it—increased focus during the mayhem of a game. Improved balance catching the ball. Improved rest to rebuild energy. Improved memory to recall the play. Sales is no different. You need focus, you need balance, you need rest, you need energy, you need memory and you need to keep your head in the game. You need to be able to EXECUTE!

WHAT – Get your brain checked out
HOW – Search "neurofeedback training"
WHEN - Now

By this time in the book, you should have a better understanding of yourself and how you get yourself into trouble. You know the reality of the chaos heading your way and you're aware of the need to embrace life-long learning. You're taking steps to minimize chaos by having everything in one place, with a process, and you are controlling your commitments better than in the past so you can spend more time in the highly productive state of flow. You have a plan for every typical sales situation so

execute

you achieve your objectives, get your customer talking and sharing their need, so you can focus more of your effort on qualified opportunities. You always have a next step so you become more productive and efficient with your limited time. You are leveraging your "good" reputation using social selling tools and your digital footprint will increase making it easier for others to cross your path. And you are doing all of this with greater energy and efficiency because you are providing fuel for your body and brain. You are focused, calm and clear. The final piece is how best to master learning new techniques, processes and skills with your new brain.

Jim Ryerson

Think It, Ink It!!

■ **WHAT**

■ **HOW**

■ **WHEN**

Submit your best practices at the link below for the chance to have it featured as a Shot of Octane Video.
https://salesoctane.com/resources/best-practices/

PROgress

VS
Perfection

Chapter 13: PROgress vs Perfection

Chapter 13

PROgress vs. Perfection

"Change itself is not PROgress, but change is the price that we pay for PROgress"

- Clayton G. Orcutt

You began reading this book with a routine. The goal was to challenge your existing routine where you would benefit from a new approach. At this point in the book you should have a number of notes at the end of each chapter defining what you want to change, how you plan to go about the change and when you plan to EXECUTE these new habits.

The challenge will be the fact that it takes a lot of effort to learn a new habit until the point where the habit becomes routine. Kanter's Law strikes again. It will get messy before it gets better which is why most salespeople just give up and revert back to their old habit. Not you, though, because you are the SalesPRO.

Go back through the end of each chapter and select three different routines you plan to EXECUTE. One of the routines should be a PROcess improvement. This could be something around your process of reducing the number of places you keep notes from Chapter 5. It could be something for your health from Chapter 12. Just pick one new business or life process you want to implement.

New Business/Life Routine

■ WHAT

One of the routines should be a technology best practice that involves the use of several key-strokes on either your computer, tablet or mobile phone. For example, it could be something as simple as how to enter a new contact into your CRM from Chapter 6. That means entering all the data your company requires. It could be something like how to set up an online screen-share meeting from Chapter 10 including sending an invitation with the details to the participant. Pick a technology task you need to learn to do or do better.

New Technology Routine

■ WHAT

Finally, one of the routines should be a new Sales Technique. For example, asking your customer for the next step at the end of one of your routine sales calls from Chapter 8. It could be how to say no to an unqualified opportunity from Chapter 9. Pick a new sales technique you need to learn to do or do better.

New Sales Technique Routine

WHAT

Step 1

What, How and When. You know why you selected the new routine, however, knowing why is never enough. We all know why we need to lose weight, start exercising, stop an addictive behavior, get up earlier or eat healthy. Why is essential but you cannot EXECUTE "why."; In order to EXECUTE, you must define the What, How and When.

Start with the new business/life routine you selected and break it down using the What, How and When approach. This is where the wisdom of taking some time to diagnose the situation and plan it out will improve the probability of a positive first step.

<u>What</u>

- What is your goal with this new routine?
- What do you need in order to EXECUTE this new routine?

- What resources, including people, will you need to pursue in order to EXECUTE this new routine?
- What are some small, incremental steps that will get the process started?

How

- How will you go about securing WHAT you need to EXECUTE?
- How will you determine where these resources or people can be found?
- How can you leverage others in this process?
- How will you keep track and reward yourself along the way?

When

- When will you make the call and gather the resources?
- When will you review your progress?
- When will you start?
- When will you finish?
- Others?

_____
_____
_____
_____

While this is not an exhaustive list of the What, How and When questions, my guess is you will find this process exhausting. And this is why habit change is so challenging. If you "just do it" by jumping in then you will likely run into an unforeseen or, shall we say, unplanned, challenge and go back to the old routine.

execute

"It's never crowded along the extra mile"

- Anon

The SalesPRO lives in the extra mile because it is the extra effort up front and at every step along the path that leads to extraordinary results.

Step 2

Take your new Technology Routine and follow the same process in Step 1 and then add a component based on how adults learn. There are many different theories on how adults learn. Visual, Kinesthetic and Auditory learning styles is one approach, which will help you understand how you might learn. There are several free tests available so simply search: "Baruch learning style test free" and get your results. My guess is auditory will not be your most dominant. This often goes along with the people-oriented extroverted tendency! We love to talk versus listen.

Other approaches for learning involve Repetition, Testing, Self-diagnosis and even having you Participate in the development of the new routine. One thing is for certain. When you are trying to learn a new technology, no one likes the person in the office who grabs your keyboard, makes a series of keystrokes, and then hands it back to you, with the confidence-draining statement, "There, it's all set, just do that the next time and it will be fine."

So, make it visual and something you can repeat down the line. With technology, the SalesPRO takes their plan from Step 1 and when they are ready to EXECUTE the new digital steps on their computer or mobile device they visually record their keystrokes and provide their commentary while recording. This way, they know exactly what to do the next time. There are numerous free solutions available for both PC and iOS which allow you to record, save and share the best practice techniques for everything you EXECUTE on any technology, whether computer, tablet or mobile phone. As a team, enlist everyone in this process. You are seldom the only one who has challenges knowing how to use all the programs and applications. And since new programs and applications are guaranteed, the SalesPRO has ONE PLACE where all the home-grown how-to videos are placed.

PROgress vs. Perfection

Step 3
    Practice...and *not on your customers!*

Q. What is the best way to learn or master a new routine?
A. Practice.

    You know you have mastered your new habit when it becomes routine. You no longer have to think about it. You simply EXECUTE.
    Next, take a look at the new sales technique you wish to master. Follow Step 1 to make sure you have a plan and have secured everything you need in order to practice. This is typically the language, your script or talking points, and any collateral materials you would use as you EXECUTE the technique. For this example, let's use the Next Step language at the end of a conversation with a new prospect.
    For step 2, because we are not executing a series of keystrokes but rather a sales technique, you need to write it out.

execute

So, write the talking points! This is hard work and here's why you may be tempted to bail.

I live on airplanes. When someone in the next seat finds out I've had the good fortune to publish a few books over the past 15 years, it's common for them to say, "I'd love to write a book!" or "I have a great idea for a book!" In either case, I inquire about their topic, how they decided they want to write a book and if I sense they are serious, I will tell them exactly how to get a book published. My parting comment as I leave the plane is, "Make sure you copy me on their first couple of tweets and blogs about the content!" I've never ever received a single one. Why?

Writing is easy. If I tell you to write the word BLUE and you write it down then you are a writer, right? Writing is purely the mechanical process of getting it from your brain to paper or text. The challenge is not writing but organizing your thoughts so you can type or write them down. This is why it is critical with every sales technique to take the time, think through the language, your "talking points," as I like to say, and write it down word-for-word. While this may look like a script, it is not! These are simply your talking points that you can practice and then use in a conversation without sounding scripted!

Once you have the words written out for the sales technique, then put it into context, meaning how it would typically flow with your customer. This begins to look like a role-play but don't worry, that is NOT what you are going to do. Context is important because it begins to orient our technique with how you will typically use it when you are talking to a customer.

Now take some time to read and re-read your lines. Much like an actor in a movie, we want to begin to burn the lines into our memory. Feel free to modify the language so it flows the way you typically speak.

Lights, Action...mobile phone. Here's the key. Role-plays are fine for the final confirmation that you have learned a technique, however, a role-play during the learning phase is the absolute fastest way to neuter a salesperson's self-confidence. The only person who wins in that exchange is the trainer, because they have mastered the lines through practice and repetition. Now they wax eloquent in front of the room as the salespeople feels inadequate, standing in the trainer's shadow.

Take your role-play scripting and practice using the video option on your mobile device. If there is a LOT of interaction between your customer and you with the technique, then have a neutral party (friend, fellow salesperson, significant other or spouse) play the role of the customer.

Start the video and keep recording as you continue to practice. Don't stop the video every time you make a mistake. Stay in flow and keep going with each take you will make progress. Once you feel like you have successfully executed the technique, then stop the video.

Watch the last take. This is called self-diagnosis, and it is the best way for you to learn. You wrote the script (participating in the development of the technique improves learning). You will make 10-15 takes before you get through the technique without using notes (repetition improves learning). You see yourself (for those visual learners), you are practicing the technique in context (for those kinesthetic learners) and you hear yourself (for those auditory learners). This is the ultimate test for mastery (yes, testing has been shown to improve learning). And all of this was done without the rest of the sales team or your manager watching. Everyone wins!

Once you are confident in your video showing mastery of the technique, you can share it with your Sales Manager or Sales Trainer as both proof of your PROficiency and as a way to solicit their insight and coaching. As a team, you can take the best videos and use them for training. Each of you has a strength and by combining the strength of each team member in a format

execute

which is easy to practice, you leverage the power of contagion![13] If a picture is worth 1,000 words, just think what a self-made video illustrating your mastery is worth?

The good news for you, the SalesPRO, is as you get more comfortable planning, organizing your thoughts and practicing mastery, you PROve to yourself why your customers are willing to recommend you to others. And this motivates you to put in the effort to learn.

Then every time you have to learn a new product or solution, a response to a new objection, a new presentation, a new technology or a new process improvement you are more proficient at these steps and they become, yes, routine.

Self-improvement begins with self. Whether you start with mastering a sales technique, process improvement, technology application or life habit the SalesPRO prepares their plan, gathers the details, leverages learning technology and puts their new skills into practice. It's time to change the way we learn so we can see our PROgress accelerate as we EXECUTE!

---

[13] https://psychology.iresearchnet.com/social-psychology/control/behavioral-contagion/

Think It, Ink It!!

■ WHAT

■ HOW

■ WHEN

Submit your best practices at the link below for the chance to have it featured as a Shot of Octane Video.
https://salesoctane.com/resources/best-practices/

PuRpOse
Essence of

– The "Good"

Chapter 14: PuRpOse – The Essence of "Good"

Chapter 14

PuRpOse – The Essence of "Good"

EXECUTE is a framework for selling in a world full of distractions, and it contains a lot of practical tips for reducing the chaos. We started with what is driving the chaos and then moved to what you can do and how to EXECUTE each technique. There was still something missing to pull it all together. And then it clicked.

When I speak at a sales conference, I offer to come in early and even stay a few days after my presentation to answer questions and learn more about their business so I can offer additional concepts or techniques. In most cases this affords the opportunity to listen to other presenters on a host of topics. There is always something to apply as a result.

While pulling the original outline together for EXECUTE, I was in the audience listening and taking notes to a speaker presenting on the topic of "purpose." I have a habit of mixing up my writing style between block letters, cursive and ALL CAPS. On one pass of the word "purpose," it jumped out at me as "PuRpOse." The word PRO is found in PuRpOse!

The dictionary defines *purpose* as:

purpose noun

pur·pose | \'per-pes\

a : the aim or goal of a person; what you are trying to do or become
b : the aim or intention of something; the reason why something is done
c : the feeling of being determined to do or achieve something

The SalesPRO is found in PuRpOse!

Step 1 – The What of PuRpOse

a : the aim or goal of a person; what you are trying to do or become | ON PURPOSE

You may believe the obvious answer to this question is hitting your sales quota. Or perhaps providing an income to sustain your lifestyle, family, etc. And while these do answer the question, I'd like to steer the conversation towards what it looks like when you, personally, are "on purpose."

In *Selling by the BOOK Today*, we identified 14 characteristics of being "good" in the sales profession. When you are "on purpose" with these characteristics, you will naturally bring value, serve your customers, solve their problems, bring solutions and give back on a daily basis.

This is a great place to begin your journey toward being *"on purpose."* Take a minute to look through the list of characteristics

execute

and put a checkmark in the box of each one where you feel confident you are *"on purpose."* Then, put a + sign in the remaining characteristics as a visual reinforcement of where you need to add some focused effort going forward

- ☐ **Likable**
- ☐ **Honest**
- ☐ **Patient**
- ☐ **Humble**
- ☐ **Generous**
- ☐ **Self-Controlled**
- ☐ **Positive Speech**

- ☐ **Listens**
- ☐ **Knowledgeable**
- ☐ **Connected**
- ☐ **Seeks Wise Counsel**
- ☐ **Organized**
- ☐ **Plans Their Work**
- ☐ **Works Their Plan**

If you have additional characteristics important to you or your product / service, market or company, add them here:

☐ _____ ☐ _____
☐ _____ ☐ _____
☐ _____ ☐ _____
☐ _____ ☐ _____
☐ _____ ☐ _____
☐ _____ ☐ _____
☐ _____ ☐ _____
☐ _____ ☐ _____

But why would you want to put forth the effort?

Step 2 – The Why of PuRpOse

b : the aim or intention of something; the reason why something is done | FOR A PURPOSE

Being "good" *and* connected is the theme of *Selling By The BOOK Today*. When you are "good," then others will talk about what you have done for them and your reputation will grow. When you are "connected," you have a robust network so your reputation will expand exponentially. Your digital tribe certainly knows you and those outside your tribe who look you up will come to the same conclusion. Why? Because it's your satisfied customers who are singing your praises.

The SalesPRO has the enviable position of giving to their customers and everyone they come in contact with on a daily basis. Why not accelerate your giving nature?

You've heard the statement, "When you give, you receive." It's true. It has been proven. You should not give in order to receive, of course, but the principle still exists. You give because you are "good" and then your customers will take care of the rest! And that is step 2 in this process. Go back and ask your customers what difference you made for them. Why do they use you, what did you do which was worthy of a referral?

> ***"Price is only an issue** when your value is in question"*
>
> *– Alan Gotthardt*

Three things will happen. First, it will be a positive reinforcement of what you are doing that is making a difference with your customer so you can build these best practices into

execute

your sales process. Success breeds success. Second, it will remind the customer of the value you bring and this reinforces their decision to continue entrusting their business to you. Remember, they said it! Third, this conversation will generate new opportunities to bring value for them and others they know, referrals.

So, if you asked your customers these questions, how would they answer?

- Why did you initially take my call?
- Why did you engage with me?
- Why did you decide to move forward with me/our company?
- What did I/we do for you/your company?
- What would you tell others about our company/me?
- OTHER:

_____

_____

_____

As mentioned in the Introduction to this book, all the predictions made in *Selling by the Book Today* in 2015 are happening. Your prospects and customers are changing roles more frequently causing your reputation to travel from one company to another. Your prospects are more suspicious of incoming cold calls. Customers share their positive and negative experiences with you and your company on social media.

Engaging with your customers with the purpose of confirming your value will not only build their confidence in you and your company but also build your confidence in your ability to EXECUTE. So, does it matter how you go about the process?

Step 3 – The How of PuRpOse

c : the feeling of being determined to do or achieve something | WITH A PURPOSE

The word *determination* generates pictures of standing atop a mountain with arms raised high, crossing a finish line victorious, emerging from a pit of mud in a Spartan race or pushing a boulder up a hill. Words like *decisive, resolved, persistent, courageous, tenacious* and *boldness* resonate with determination. The question we need to answer is how, how will you unleash your determination?

Sales is the easiest low-paying job
Sales is the hardest high-paying job

Sales is hard work when you are determined to become the SalesPRO. Motivation to put in the extraordinary effort occurs when your customers reinforce you are doing "good" which is why you need to routinely ask them the questions in Step 2. As you give you receive in many different ways including referrals, which will happen more often when you are "good," which is why we routinely hone the 14 characteristics in step 1.

*"**Every day we get closer** to or farther from our target"*

– Jim Ryerson

We all make mistakes. We live in a world of chaos. To suggest I EXECUTE flawlessly every day in every situation would be a lie.

I am human. I routinely make mistakes and fail to EXECUTE, including the values I profess. Life is a journey and the journey never ends. The key question is what do you do when you fall short?

*"**Bitter** or better, the only two options"*

– Jim Ryerson

These two words often define the fundamental difference between those who improve over time from those who keep getting stuck and move from one failed event to another. You *will* experience failed events. Now, the words "failed event" have been chosen carefully and are critical for the SalesPRO. People are not failures, they simply experience failed events. A series of failed events often begin to define a person both to themselves and the outside world. The key is to EXECUTE quickly and break the cycle. It begins with the choice between Bitter and Better.

"Those who master change persist and persevere."

- Rosabeth Moss Kanter

When you experience a failed event, it is essential to avoid the blame game. Instead, take accountability and move forward. If you have to be bitter, get it out of your system fast as you will not improve until you do! Move forward and ask yourself this question, "What would I do differently if I had a similar situation in the future?" Because there is a good chance that if you don't change something, you will have a similar situation in the future. That's the beauty of embracing Better vs. Bitter. Each failed event is a critical point to get better and improve as a SalesPRO.

Be on purpose, for a purpose, with a purpose and before long you will prosper!

execute

Think It, Ink It!!

■ **WHAT**

■ **HOW**

■ **WHEN**

Submit your best practices at the link below for the chance to have it featured as a Shot of Octane Video.
https://salesoctane.com/resources/best-practices/

The Will

SalesPRO
PROsper

Chapter 15: The SalesPRO Will PROsper

Chapter 15

The SalesPRO Will PROsper

How do you end a book when the topic has no end? The motivating factor to EXECUTE is change. And, as the saying goes, "The only constant is change."

As we've covered in both this book and *Selling by The BOOK Today*, the world we live in will change more rapidly with each generation. With each change comes the decision of what it means to you and how you must modify your routine. Your company, product and service evolves in response to market changes, and as a result you must learn new techniques, systems and language. Knowledge increases at an escalating rate, requiring you to both learn and apply the learning to your situation.

You change personally as you gain a better understanding of how you are wired, your behaviors, motivations and values. Every new insight into who you are provides an opportunity to change your actions so you can better leverage your strengths and adapt where improvements are needed. Finally, your personal situation will change as you move through different seasons in life. Yes, the only thing constant is change.

I ended the Preface at the start of this book with same statement I use at the close of every presentation, webinar, Shot Of Octane™ video and workshop: "See you at the finish line!" The challenge is, the finish line keeps moving! So, what will keep *you* moving?

The word PROsper means different things to different people. In the world of sales it typically brings to mind PROsperity driven by sales revenue, commissions and income.

The Pareto Principle, coined by Management consultant Joseph M. Juran in 1896, is often referred to as the 80/20 rule[14]. This principle is used to suggest such ideas as:

- 20% of the sales force (the SalePRO's) will take 80% of the income
- 80% of the sales force will split the remaining 20% of the income (ouch)

What if the Pareto Principle is wrong and before long 5% of the sales force will accumulate 95% of the income?

For others PROsperity means selling something they enjoy. They PROsper simply by being able to do what they love and see the difference they make in the lives of their customers and colleagues.

Still others may have picked up this book because they live in a world of chaos and just want to gain clarity, focus and balance.

What if you could achieve all three? What if you could do what you love, the money would follow and you achieved this with balance in your life?

That is the PuRpOse of this book.

---

[14] https://betterexplained.com/articles/understanding-the-pareto-principle-the-8020-rule/

execute

So, I leave you with some targets as you begin this life-long journey as the SalesPRO and I intend to run the race with you whether it's on Shot Of Octane™, a WEBinar, at your sales convention or at www.salesoctane.com/resources/EXECUTE:

- Apply yourself to learning (PROfessor of Sales)
- Move everything to ONE Place (PROgram & PROcess)
- Always do what you say you will do (PROmise)
- Plan before you "just do it" (PROactive)
- Learn to say "no" (PRiOrity)
- Spend your time and energy on ideal customers (PRObability)
- Spend more time in flow (PROduce)
- Prospect to referrals (PROspect)
- Build your social selling reputation (PROmote)
- Take care of your body and brain (PROvide)
- Practice mastery and share your learning (PROgress)
- Spend more time doing what you love (on PuRpOse)
- And you will PROsper!

These are lofty targets but you are the SalesPRO. Let's EXECUTE!

See you at the finish line!

Jim Ryerson

Think It, Ink It!!

■ WHAT

■ HOW

■ WHEN

Submit your best practices at the link below for the chance to have it featured as a Shot of Octane Video.
https://salesoctane.com/resources/best-practices/

Acknowledgements

Over the course of writing this book, I kept a digital journal and penned down the names of the people I interviewed. Whenever I would have a spontaneous conversation that resulted in a revelation, I would add their name. The challenge is this journey began long before the diagnosis in June, 2017. I know there are many individuals who have impacted me in the area of focus, productivity, habits and self-improvement prior to beginning this book. You know who you are, and I thank you for your contribution and extend my apologies for not including you in this edit. Please let me know and I will add you in a future printing! Think it, Ink it!

Scott Riffel, Project Outbox, you keep me and so many others on track. Harry, as always, not only do you dominate every board game you also have mastered the English language. Chris McMorrow, you are the most creative person with graphics I have ever met. The remainder are in alphabetical order: Dr. Ravin Bastiampillai, Nick Bolhuis, Ken Bowman, Brains Potential Team, Rob Bunke, Arthur Chou, John Dickson, Stan Felder, Rochelle Fintelman, LMSW, BCN, Robal Johnson, Rick Kuiper, Rob Langejans, Bennett Mallory, Jeff Manion, Buz Mayo, Carol Mettenbrink, Mark Murrison, Samantha Neugebauer, LLMSW, BCN, Notes Plus Team, Jesse J. Piehl, PhD, David Reid, Russ Rymal, Scott Sandberg, Don Sanders, Jim Stull, Target Training International Team, Dr. David Thompson, Viet Tran, Brian Upton, Harold VanEerden, Gary VanDyke, Elyse White, PhD and Mike Wiersema.

Biography

Jim Ryerson is the founder and Chief Acceleration Officer of Sales Octane, Inc., a group of individuals dedicated to helping others apply time-honored principles to grow themselves, their sales and their business.

Jim started his career in sales with one of the top 25 sales forces in the country as ranked by Sales and Marketing magazine. Jim dedicates himself to learning how behavioral styles, motivation, competencies and mastery combine to help salespeople become sales *professionals*!

Diane Lee Photography

Made in the USA
Columbia, SC
24 January 2019